# Cambridge Elements ≡

Elements in Language Teaching
edited by
Heath Rose
*Linacre College, University of Oxford*
Jim McKinley
*University College London*

# LANGUAGE TEACHER EDUCATOR IDENTITY

Gary Barkhuizen
*University of Auckland*

CAMBRIDGE
UNIVERSITY PRESS

# CAMBRIDGE
## UNIVERSITY PRESS

University Printing House, Cambridge CB2 8BS, United Kingdom

One Liberty Plaza, 20th Floor, New York, NY 10006, USA

477 Williamstown Road, Port Melbourne, VIC 3207, Australia

314–321, 3rd Floor, Plot 3, Splendor Forum, Jasola District Centre, New Delhi – 110025, India

79 Anson Road, #06–04/06, Singapore 079906

Cambridge University Press is part of the University of Cambridge.

It furthers the University's mission by disseminating knowledge in the pursuit of education, learning, and research at the highest international levels of excellence.

www.cambridge.org
Information on this title: www.cambridge.org/9781108812665
DOI: 10.1017/9781108874083

First published 2021

*A catalogue record for this publication is available from the British Library.*

ISBN 978-1-108–81266-5 Paperback
ISSN 2632-4415 (online)
ISSN 2632-4407 (print)

# Language Teacher Educator Identity

Elements in Language Teaching

DOI: 10.1017/9781108874083
First published online: February 2021

Gary Barkhuizen
*University of Auckland*

**Author for correspondence:** Gary Barkhuizen, g.barkhuizen@auckland.ac.nz

**Abstract:** The author examines who language teacher educators are in the field of language teaching and learning. This includes a description of the different types of language teacher educators working in a range of professional and institutional contexts, an analysis of the reflections of a group of experienced English teacher educators working in Colombia and enrolled in a doctoral programme to continue their professional development, and an exposition of the work that language teacher educators do, particularly in the domains of pedagogy, research, and service and leadership (institutional and community). All of this is done with the aim of understanding the identities that language teacher educators negotiate and are ascribed in their working contexts. The author emphasizes the need for research to pay attention to the lives and work of language teacher educators, and offers forty research questions as an indication of possible future research directions.

**Keywords:** language teacher educator, identity

ISBNs: 9781108812665 (PB), 9781108874083 (OC)
ISSNs: ISSN 2632-4415 (online), ISSN 2632-4407 (print)

# Contents

# 1 Who Are Language Teacher Educators?

It sounds simple enough – *language teacher educators teach teachers how to teach language*. But when we think about this sentence more deeply questions immediately begin to emerge. For example:

1 Who are these teachers learning to teach language? Have they ever taught before; that is, are they pre-service teachers, or do they already have some teaching experience?
2 Who are the teacher educators? How do they teach the teachers? How much experience do they actually have as classroom language teachers? What other professional responsibilities do they have; for example, doing research, managing a department, advocating for policy change? What are their qualifications to become teacher educators?
3 What exactly do the educators teach the pre-service or in-service teachers? What does language teacher education pedagogy look like? Is it all about language teaching methodology – what to do in the classroom? What is the place of theory? What about social justice education?
4 Is the language to be taught the first language of the student teachers, or an additional language, or one of many languages in the particular teaching/ learning context? How proficient in this language or these languages are the teachers and the teacher educator? Does it matter?
5 Do language teacher educators reflect on their practice?
6 Is there a knowledge-base of language teacher education? What does it consist of?

These questions focus on three core domains. The first of these relates to the teachers who are learning to teach or who are continuing their professional development. They are the central characters in the language teacher education enterprise, and this is reflected in the relatively large literature that deals with second or foreign language teacher education, including empirical studies, teacher education textbooks, and specialist handbooks and edited compilations. This work aims to examine and understand how teachers learn to become teachers, what they know when they know how to teach, how they continue to develop professionally over time, and how their teacher identities relate to what they do, both inside and outside the classroom.

The second core domain raised by the questions has to do with the content and pedagogy of language teacher education. This refers to what is taught to teachers and what they learn in the process of their teacher education. It includes how the process of this teaching and learning unfolds and why. There is no preferred description or universal explanation of this process, and there is no one set of recommendations for how it should be done. There are two obvious reasons for this: one is that the contexts of teacher education – regional, political, economic, institutional – are infinitely varied globally, and two, these contexts, as well as the disciplinary field of language education more generally, are constantly evolving. Language, of course, is central to the process of language teacher education, not only as the subject matter that is taught by teachers, but also as the medium through which they are taught to teach that language or languages by teacher educators. Labels such as 'first', 'second', 'native', 'foreign', and 'additional' applied to these languages reflects the varied and changing nature as well as the complexity of the teacher education landscape.

The third core domain involves the teacher educators. In language teacher education, educators can vary from those who have very little classroom experience, if any at all, to those who are deeply connected to classroom life, either through their own concurrent practice and employment as a language teacher, or through the supervision or mentoring of student teachers during their teaching practice (practicum), for example. Language teacher educators teach (prospective) language teachers, and their pedagogy is a major constituent of the work they do as educators. But it is not all. They are also involved in scholarly activities, such as reading and doing research, participating in work-shops and conferences, and even studying for further qualifications. In addition, they typically engage in the interests of professional associations and take part in policy discussions in order to keep up with and contribute to developments in the language education field, sometimes locally within a particular institution or region but also more widely.

These three core domains – the language teachers, the content and peda-gogy of teacher education, and the teacher educators – are significant con-stituents of the knowledge-base of language teacher education (LTE), however it may be defined. In reflecting on past conceptualizations of this knowledge-base, Johnson and Golombek (2020) point out that a major omis-sion in its focus has been 'what teacher educators do', in other words, 'LTE pedagogy'. They argue that LTE pedagogy needs to 'be recognized as a central domain in the knowledge-base of LTE' (p. 117). They elaborate on what this entails:

> Greater attention to LTE pedagogy means making explicit not just what teacher educators ask teachers to do in their teacher education programs but what we do, as teacher educators; our goals, intentions, expectations, the quality and character of our pedagogy, and the consequences of our pedagogy on the ways in which teachers come to understand both the scope and impact of their teaching. (p. 117)

This proposal clearly positions *teacher educators* and their work as vitally integral to the activity of language teacher education. Others too have decried the lack of attention paid to teacher educators in language teacher education scholarship. Trent (2013) says straightforwardly that teacher educators 'have not been thoroughly researched' (p. 262), and others concur (Farrell, 2015; Kani, 2014; Wood & Borg, 2010; Wright, 2010), including Peercy et al. (2019) who say, 'We currently know relatively little about teacher educators as learners and as reflective scholars open to examining their own practice and research' (p. 2). This latter comment adds a further dimension to our lack of knowledge regarding teacher educators; that is, how they (those that do) go about exploring or self-reflecting on their own work as educators.

Despite this apparent deficiency in knowledge about language teacher educators, efforts have been made to uncover their autobiographical experiences (Casanave & Schecter, 1997) and qualities (Moradkhani et al., 2013), and more recently Farrell (2015) collated personal descriptions of the work and programmes of teacher educators in various international contexts. Maley (2019) invited twenty very experienced professionals, most working as teacher educators for many years, to reflect on their personal histories, including the places they have worked, the people they met along the way, and critical moments in their own development. And a recent issue of *TESOL Journal* (Lindahl & Yazan, 2019) included a number of research-based articles focussing specifically on English teacher educators.

The overdue recommendation to focus on teacher educators means by necessity that our gaze shifts to who the educators are – their history, their beliefs, experiences, roles and practices, emotions and desires, and their moral stance. In other words, their language teacher educator *identity*, or more accurately, their multiple identities. This represents yet another aspect of language teacher educators' lives that remains underexplored and surprisingly invisible. As Yazan (2018) asserts, language teacher educator identity 'is still undertheorized and underresearched' (p. 141). This Element is about the identity of language teacher educators. I attempt to describe who language teacher educators are. Gee's (2000) well-known and seemingly straightforward definition of identity claims that identity is 'being recognized as a certain "kind of person", in a given context' (p. 99). The questions that guide my discussion include, therefore: what kind of people are language teacher educators, in the professional contexts in which they work? How are they recognized as language teacher educators? How do they learn to become teacher educators, and how do they grow as educators? Identity, of course, means not only how people are perceived by others, but also how they see themselves – their own reflexive understanding of who they are. To address this dimension of identity, I draw on interview data from a study that explored the shifting identities of experienced language teacher educators, *from their perspectives*, as they transition through further study.

## 1.1 The Aim and Organization of This Element

This Element has five main sections:

1  In this first section I introduce the topic: language teacher educator identity. I ask who language teacher educators are, and provide examples of the types of professionals who work as teacher educators. I also provide some working definitions of concepts to be used in later sections, including some published definitions of 'teacher educator'.

2  The second section introduces a study I conducted with teacher educators in Colombia, which I will refer to in later sections as well. In this section, brief excerpts from narrative interviews illustrate the educators' understandings of their own changing teacher educator identities. Main themes from their reflections are extracted and discussed.

3  In Section 3 I ask: what do language teacher educators do? Having established in the first two sections who language teacher educators are, this section explores the pedagogical work of teacher educators in relation to their perceived identities. To address this broad question, I use the eight propositions that Johnson and Golombek (2020) suggest constitute LTE pedagogy as a central domain for the knowledge-base of teacher education, and do so from the teacher educators' perspective, focussing particularly on their identity construction. To support the propositions, I draw on concepts from a study by Hacker (2008) that explored the learning of language teacher educators.

4  Section 4 then considers why language teacher educators decide to continue their professional development. It returns to findings from the Colombian study. Here, I explore the reasons why the teacher educator participants decided to enrol in a doctoral programme, and how this decision intersected with their investment (Norton, 2013) in further education and the negotiation of their identities.

5  The final section concludes the Element by considering avenues for future research in the area of language teacher educator identity. Based on the previous four sections, I suggest topics for research and include related, specific research questions.

The five sections, then, follow a logical sequence of first introducing who language teacher educators are, then examining their reflections on their identities, followed by a discussion of the work they do in relation to their identities, an exploration of their reasons for deciding to continue their education, and then ending with questions for further research. In each section, I include one or two brief personal narratives from my career as a language teacher and teacher educator. The narratives serve to position me as author of the Element, generally and in relation to the content being discussed at the time. I hope that they are both interesting and informative.

Having outlined the content of this Element, here is a note about what it does not cover. This falls into two main areas. The first has to do with the process of language teacher education – how it is or should be done. In other words, this is not a textbook about second language teacher education, its pedagogies and curriculums, or the design of its programmes. In a sense, though, it is about all of these, but only insofar as they relate to the identities of the people pivotal to the teacher education process – the teacher educators.

The second area not covered in this Element is theories of identity. This Element is not the place to repeat these theoretical positions and would distract from its main purpose, that is, to present in some detail an overview of the identities of language teacher educators by addressing the question: what kind of people are language teacher educators, in the professional contexts in which they work? Nevertheless, I include a brief statement here of some of the more prominent theories. Conceptualizations of identity – what identity is, different epistemological perspectives – and particularly *teacher* identity, have in recent years been covered quite extensively elsewhere in the literature (Barkhuizen, 2017; De Costa & Norton, 2017; Gray & Morton, 2018; Varghese et al., 2016; Yazan & Lindahl, 2020). The range of perspectives, reflected in methodological approaches to investigate identity, include poststructural orientations such as Norton's (2013) notion of investment in relation to the theories of Bourdieu, identification within communities of practice (Canagarajah, 2017; Trent, 2013), identity-in-discourse (Varghese, 2017), identity-as-practice (Morgan, 2004), critical realism (Block, 2013), and theories of race, colonialism, and empire (Motha, 2014). De Costa and Norton (2017) draw on the work of the Douglas Fir Group (2016) to propose a transdisciplinary approach to language teacher identity in the introductory article of a special issue of *The Modern Language Journal*, which includes six contributions that cover topics such as how teacher identity intersects with the multilingual and translingual realities of contemporary classrooms, the investment of teachers in developing the semiotic repertoires of learners and a socially inclusive learning environment, and the emotions and ethical practices of teachers. Following a transdisciplinarity agenda, and drawing on a range of different theories in conceptualizing teacher identity, the studies take into account the highly inter-related macro-, meso-, and micro-level dimensions of language teaching and learning. De Costa and Norton (2017) note in their discussion that 'there is much evidence to support the view that language teaching is indeed "identity work" and that language teaching is enhanced by effective teacher training, both inservice and preservice' (p. 11).

This final comment raises two matters pertinent to this Element. The first is that language teaching is identity work (Miller, Morgan, & Medina, 2017); the self-formation of being and becoming a teacher in the practice of doing teaching. The same applies, of course, to language teacher educators. Doing teacher education is identity work. Who individuals are as teacher educators, including their past and imagined future identities, affects their pedagogies and all other aspects of their teacher education work, and at the same time their practices constantly change who they are and desire to be. This relates to the second matter regarding De Costa and Norton's comment: that language teaching is enhanced by effective teacher training. Once again language teacher educators (trainers) are vitally positioned in the language teaching/learning enterprise, as Vanassche and Kelchtermans (2016) also remind us, 'teacher educators are key to educational systems . . . as they strongly impact the quality of teaching and learning in our schools' (p. 355).

To end this introduction, I briefly define a few terms so that for the following sections we are all on the same page, so to speak. These are not particularly controversial, though they have been defined differently by various scholars, and even the same scholars have changed their ideas about them over time. The three terms I wish to clarify are as follows, and I am guided by the distinction that Freeman (2016) makes:

1 *Language teacher education*: this is the superordinate term describing a process that serves like a bridge 'to link what is known in the field with what is done in the classroom, and it does so through the individuals whom we educate as teachers' (Freeman, 1989, p. 30). 'We' here refers to teacher educators who are the subject of interest in this Element, and the 'individuals' are pre-service or in-service teachers who learn to teach and learn about teaching. Freeman (2016) expands the description of language teacher education as follows: 'To describe the connecting, building, and refining of knowledge and know-how through formal processes of professional preparation and further development' (p. 9).

2 *(Continuous) professional development*: as a type of language teacher education, professional development is focussed on the teacher learner and less directly on any particular 'intervention' (see *teacher training* in the next point). Freeman (2016) cites Day (1999) who says, 'Professional

development consists of all natural learning experiences and those conscious and planned activities [workshops, conferences, formal study] which are intended to be of direct or indirect benefit to the individual, group or school' (p. 9).

3 *Teacher training*: as a second type of teacher education, training involves more direct intervention – it is specific, focussed, and timely (Freeman, 2016, p. 8). Richards and Farrell (2005) add that it involves activities where the goals are immediate to short term and relate to a teacher's current teaching circumstances, whether that be preparing for a first teaching position or a new situation as a more experienced practitioner.

One might say, at the risk of over-simplifying matters, that training focusses on providing teachers in preparation with practical skills to operate in the classroom, whereas professional development aims to enable teachers to develop a broader knowledge-base, including relevant theory and the ability to self-reflect and to engage with and in research; both being teacher education and not always easily distinguishable. (See also Bolitho, 2020, who exemplifies this distinction when he describes differences between initial certificate courses and higher education courses.)

## 1.2 Who Are Language Teacher Educators?

This section starts with my first personal narrative. The aim of this one is to introduce one kind of language teacher educator – one who is teaching without any intention of actually being a teacher educator, but might just marginally be so. After briefly discussing the narrative, I give further examples of more obvious language teacher educators.

PERSONAL NARRATIVE 1: STARTING TO TEACH

My first formal teaching experience was as a graduate teaching assistant at university. In my institution we were called tutors. At the time I was a BA Honours student (a post-BA graduate qualification) in the linguistics department at Rhodes University in South Africa. My degree included papers in sociolinguistics, the history of the English language, Anglo-Saxon literature, and methods and assessment in second language teaching. At this university, students who studied English literature in their first year were required to take modules in linguistics, and so were taught in lectures and small group tutorials by members of the linguistics department. My teaching job was to contribute to the tutorials. Each week I'd facilitate about four or five groups of around fifteen students, usually repeating the same material in all tutorials in any particular week.

Topics ranged from introductory syntax and phonetics, to language and society, and discourse analysis. It is probably true that many of the students sitting in these tutorials were going to become English teachers, although that need not have been the case – there were many other available majors at the university that allowed a course or two of English in their curriculums. Many of these latter students probably ended up becoming English teachers anyway, even though that might not have been their intention at the start of their studies. However, the focus of the tutorials was definitely linguistics, and not teaching or pedagogy. I conducted tutorials in this programme for one academic year.

In this narrative, I was not being a teacher educator – at least not on purpose. I suppose one could argue that for those students who intended to become teachers, I was serving some teacher educator role by delivering content relevant to their future work as English teachers, what has been called disciplinary knowledge (see Freeman, Webre, & Epperson, 2019). These early preservice English teachers might have been listening to me talking about linguistics subject matter and even learning something about linguistics. They might also have been making connections with their imagined future practice as English teachers. But that would not have been because of me intentionally functioning as a language teacher educator. My unintentional identity as a teacher educator in that particular role, therefore, might be perceived to be on one extreme end of a teacher educator identity continuum (perhaps even further towards this non-teacher-educator end of the continuum would be the situation where the English literature students in the tutorials did not intend becoming teachers, but did anyway!), with more clear-cut definitions of language teacher educator being positioned towards the other end; for example, teacher educators working in institutions of higher education (in an education department), with the specific professional job description of preparing teachers to teach, and may themselves even be concurrently practising as language teachers.

It would be an impossible task to attempt to classify the different types of language teacher educators working around the world. There are just too many variables to take into account. For example, on a macro level one would need to consider national political systems, educational systems and related policies, sociocultural practices, sociolinguistic landscapes and language policies, and economic conditions (Hayes, 2005; Motteram & Dawson, 2019). At the micro level, what goes on in regions, communities, institutions, and classrooms reflects these macro-level variables, and is typically evident in the institutional and other professional roles language teacher educators play, their place of work and the facilities and conditions there, and what they actually do in their practices (Padwad & Parnham, 2019; Teemant, 2020). Nevertheless, below I give examples of different types of language teacher educators, based mainly on the roles they play and the work they do in their particular contexts, in order to illustrate the scope of their work and the kinds of professional people they are (Gee, 2000). As I've just said, this list is not exhaustive, but certainly captures the core aspects of their work and identities as language teacher educators. I believe anyone who identifies as a language teacher educator would be able to place themselves in one (or close to one, or more than one) of the fourteen categories. For each type I give the following information: (a) their teacher educator role, which may be institutionally designated; (b) place of work, or institution; (c) what professional work they do, very much like a job description; (d) potential self-identity description, or how they might perceive their identities as teacher educators; and (e) relevant references that address or directly research the particular type of teacher educator.

1  *Role*:  **Academic leader**
   *Where*:  Higher education institution, such as university or college of education.
   –  Do minimal teaching.
   –  Perform management roles such as head of a department, dean of a faculty, or leader of a team.
   –  Minimally active in research related to their academic discipline.

These academics might identify as former teacher educators, and possibly still do, but would not have been in a language classroom for some time. They primarily see themselves as managers or leaders in institutions where teacher education takes place. *References*: De Stefani (2019); Shah (2017).

2  *Role*:  **Academic position**
   *Where*:  Higher education institution, typically a university.
   –  Teach content courses such as linguistics, literature, sociolinguistics, discourse analysis (not necessarily for teachers).
   –  Engage actively in research in their fields of expertise, not related to language teaching.

These academics would not identify as teacher educators, and would not be involved in language schools or other teacher education activities. They see themselves as specialists in their academic subjects, and may not even be aware that pre- or in-service teachers are sitting in their classes. *References*: Billot (2010); Smith et al. (2016).

3  *Role*:    **Academic teacher educator position**
   *Where*:   Higher education institution, university, or college of
             education.
   –         Teach courses that are relevant to pre- and in-service teachers,
             such as teaching methods, second language acquisition, lan-
             guage assessment.
   –         Engage actively in research in these same areas.

The teaching and research of these academics is closely applicable to language teaching and teachers, and they would see themselves as teacher educators. Though some may identify more as researchers, with little contact with teachers in schools. *References*: Golombek (2017); Maley (2019).

4  *Role*:    **Teacher educator position**
   *Where*:   Higher education institution, university, or college of
             education.
   –         Hired specifically as a teacher educator.
   –         Teach relevant teacher education courses.
   –         Supervise student teacher (action) research.
   –         Supervise students during their internship or practicum
             experience.
   –         Do no or very little research.

These teacher educators identify strongly as teacher educators, though they also seek professional credibility from their former (or current) language teacher identity, which they do not want to give up, thus creating identity conflicts. They may feel marginalized if their institutions do not recognize or legitimize their institutional status. *References*: Al-Issa (2017); Kani (2014).

5  *Role*:    **Academic and supervisor of student research**
   *Where*:   Higher education institution, typically a university.
   –         May do some teaching in areas relevant to the teacher educa-
             tion programme, but minimal.
   –         Main academic activity is supervising graduate student
             research (Master's and particularly doctoral).
   –         Supervise limited if any undergraduate research.
   –         Highly active researchers in area of expertise.

These teacher educators work with experienced teachers who are seeking further qualifications. They do not see themselves as classroom-focussed in their work, but identify as skilled academic researchers and supervisors of high-level academic research. *References*: Bégin and Gérard (2013); Halse (2011).

6  *Role*:    **Teacher trainer**
    *Where*:  College of education or private teacher training institution (or school-based).
    –     Work directly face-to-face or online with pre-service teachers participating in their initial teacher training.
    –     Teach content that is close to classroom practice.
    –     Tend to focus on own development of teaching methodology and skills.
    –     Observe and assess teaching practice and micro-teaching.

Trainers identify with and as practitioners. They see themselves as situated in the language classroom and knowledgeable about what to do there. They may attend workshops and teaching-focussed conferences, and may engage in self-reflection, but otherwise do not typically identify as formal researchers or academic scholars. *References*: Motteram and Dawson (2019); Wright and Bolitho (2007).

7  *Role*:    **Mentor of teacher research**
    *Where*:  Higher education institution, university, or college of education.
    –     Work closely with teacher-researchers in schools, usually one-on-one or in small groups.
    –     Develop teacher-researchers' research skills.
    –     Provide emotional and professional support.
    –     Teach relevant courses in addition to mentoring, and carry out own (practitioner) research.

Mentors identify as caring collaborators working closely with teacher-researchers. They strive to maintain equal power relationships and desire attributes such as guide, helper, supporter, and collaborator. In their institutions they are also active teachers, and may carry out research, which would be directly related to teacher education and might not always be appreciated as 'academic enough' by the institution. *References*: Békés (2020); Smith (2020).

8  *Role*:    **Mentor for teachers on internship or practicum**
    *Where*:  Higher education institution, university, or college of education.
    –     Develop teachers' practical classroom skills.
    –     Observe and assess teaching practice.

– Manage the programme collaboration between school and higher education institution.
– Liaise with school's co-operating teacher (see point 11).
– Teach relevant courses in addition to mentoring, and carry out own research.

Mentors of teachers on internships or practicums probably have other teacher educator roles, such as teacher, potentially a researcher, and administrative co-ordinator of the internship or practicum programme, thus negotiating multiple identities. However, some might be hired in institutions mainly or exclusively as a practicum mentor, and they would more strongly identify with this role. *References*: Nguyen (2017); Yazan (2018).

9  *Role*:  **Mentor for in-service teachers in schools**
   *Where*:  Higher education institution, university, or college of education.
– Work on collaborative research project, teaching, or curriculum innovation, or policy implementation.
– Manage the collaboration between school and higher education institution.
– Liaise and organize regular meetings with school-based team members for duration of project.
– Teach relevant courses in addition to mentoring, and carry out own research.

Mentors of in-service language teachers in schools working on specific projects identify as facilitators or consultants with the relevant knowledge and experience. The members of the 'team' bring different skills and personal qualities to the project. The mentors also have teacher educator and researcher roles in their institutions. *References*: Brancard and QuinnWilliams (2012); Clarke (2019).

10  *Role*:  **School-based teacher educator**
    *Where*:  Based in the institution that teaches language – a school.
– Released from regular teaching duties (to some extent) to mentor student teachers (interns).
– Observe teaching and provide feedback.
– Provide emotional support.
– Function as model teacher.
– Induct student teacher into institutional and professional life.

Mentors potentially identify as 'parent' or 'guardian', and also as role model. They are seen by the institution and self-identify as expert teachers, with more experience and the ability to establish and sustain collegial collaborations on multiple levels, including personal and institutional. *References*: Bullough (2005); Grassick (2019).

11   *Role*:   **Co-operating teacher**
      *Where*:  Based in the institution that teaches language – a school.
- Host student teacher in their classroom and school while continuing regular teaching duties.
- Are observed teaching by student teacher.
- Observe student teacher and provide critical feedback, as well as encouragement and support.
- Liaise with teacher educator from student teacher's institution.

Co-operating teachers are based in schools or language-learning institutions and continue regular teaching, and so identify primarily as teacher practitioners. They see themselves as critical supporters of student teachers with appropriate levels of expertise, responsibility, and institutional knowledge. *References*: Farrell (2008); Yan and He (2010).

12   *Role*:   **Graduate teaching assistant**
      *Where*:  Higher education institution, typically a university.
- Assist university academics teaching a class (or, more rarely, solely responsible for own class), which will be more or less language education focussed.
- Plan course content, though usually to a limited extent.
- Assess student teacher work.
- Do associated administrative tasks.

Teaching assistants are graduate students and this is their primary identity at the time. They have no or little language teaching experience, though some may be considerably experienced, especially if studying for a doctoral-level qualification. Teaching assistants may experience tensions among their multiple identities, with internal and external power struggles, including those involving their student teachers and their professors. *References*: Wang and Mantero (2018); Yazan (2019).

13   *Role*:   **Teacher educator and language teacher**
      *Where*:  Higher education institution, university, or college of education – and language school.

- Perform teacher educator functions at higher education institution.
- Concurrently, teach language in the same institution or in a different language school.

These professionals have two main roles at the same time, language teacher educator and language teacher, and may even be employed in two different institutions. Their identities would reflect this complex mix of roles, duties, and loyalties, and may create quite stressful identity dilemmas for them. *References*: Vaillant (2011).

14  *Role*:    **Teacher of English or of English for specific or academic purposes**

*Where*:   Higher education institution, university, or college of education.

- Teach general English classes for students at the institution, some of whom may become language teachers.
- Teach English for Specific or Academic Purposes to students at the institution, some of whom may become language teachers.
- Perform some or all tasks associated with full- or part-time language teaching, such as course design, lesson planning, material writing, and assessment.

These practitioners identify as language teachers, either of general English or English for specific or academic purposes, within their higher educational institutions. Some may engage in practitioner research, or collaborate with academic researchers, but they would not claim a researcher identity (and would typically not be paid to do research). *References*: Nagatomo (2012); Van Lankveld et al. (2017).

## 1.3 Definitions of Language Teacher Educators

The section above exemplifies the scope of professionals who identify as or who might be recognized as language teacher educators. As I have cautioned, the fourteen categories are only a partial representation of types of language teacher educator, since many contextual factors inevitably mean that considerable variation exists. Broadly speaking, however, they do have significant character-istics in common. For the purposes of their study, Goodwin et al. (2014) define teacher educators as 'university-based, doctoral prepared faculty who engage in teacher educating – that is, the preparation of preservice or future teachers'

(p. 300). This is also the case with most of the language teacher educator types outlined above, but Goodwin et al. do go on, at least from the perspective of the United States, to acknowledge that:

> many field- and school-based educators also participate in teacher education (such as cooperating teachers and field supervisors), and that in recent years, there has been an exponential rise in school-based or other alternate teacher preparation programs resulting in a concomitant increase in individuals who hold the title 'teacher educator'. However, the majority of new teachers are still prepared by university-based programs, and tenure-line faculty holding doctorates remain the primary architects of these state-approved programs that lead to initial certification. (p. 300)

This extension captures some of the other types of teacher educators in the fourteen categories, but not all, and, as I've said, there are no doubt other types as well.

The following selection of definitions of 'teacher educator' taken from the literature on both language and general education illustrate some of the broad commonalities across all the educator types.

1 Amott and Ang (2020) define a teacher educator as 'any education professional working to support the professional learning of teachers, whether they be student teachers, newly qualified teachers, or experienced teachers' (p. 1). In this definition, teachers with all levels of teaching experience are included, and educators are designated as supporters of the teachers' learning, which the authors refer to as 'professional' learning.

2 Lunenberg, Dengerink, and Korthagen (2014) also refer to 'supporting' when they describe what teacher educators do, and they define them as 'all those who teach or coach (student) teachers with the aim of supporting their professional development' (p. 6). They speak of professional 'development' rather than professional learning, and use the concept 'coach', which has connotations of training, as opposed to education (see my definitions of these concepts in Section 1.1 above).

3 With specific reference to language teacher educators, Moradkhani et al. (2013) define teacher educators as 'those professionals who provide formal instruction and support for both teacher candidates and practising teachers during pre-service and/or in-service teacher education/training programs' (p. 124). Once again the role of support is mentioned in this definition, alongside 'formal instruction', which emphasizes the systematic nature of the teacher education process. They also include pre- and in-service teachers, and cover both education and training situations.

4 Peercy and Sharkey (2020) assign three identities to their definition of language teacher educator, 'as scholar, as practitioner, as researcher' (p. 106).

These will be explored in more detail later, but briefly and simply: scholar is the academic identity that engages in the pursuit of knowledge relevant to language teaching and learning; practitioner relates to language teaching pedagogy and know-how, with regard to both (student) teachers and the teacher educators themselves; and researcher identifies the teacher educator as being active in research, to actively pursue current and relevant knowledge.

5 Finally, Yazan (2018) also includes the researcher component of the teacher educators' role and identity, and adds that this aspect of their work is typically an institutional requirement: 'Teacher educators also identify themselves as academics or researchers in most cases, because research productivity is typically a key component in their professional responsibilities framed by institutional norms' (p. 144).

These broad definitions provide a backdrop to the language teacher educator reflections in the next section. In the reflections, the educators talk about how they perceive their teacher educator identities. Finer details of what it means to be a *language* teacher educator very quickly emerge.

## 2 Teacher Educators Reflecting on Their Identity

In this section, I draw on data from a study that explored the identity experiences of a group of seven teacher educators, four males and three females, enrolled in a doctoral programme at a public university in Colombia, South America. The teacher educators formed a cohort of students, meaning that they start the programme together, work their way through the required coursework, and participate in an overseas internship together before embarking on their dissertation research independently. The aim of the study was to explore the construction of their teacher educator identities within the institutional structures of the doctoral programme, as well as more broadly over their professional experience within the context of the education system in Colombia. I introduce the study in this section since I will be discussing it further in Section 4 below. I then give examples of statements the educators make about the kind of language teacher educator they are – reflecting their identity, and at the same time illustrating aspects of the definitions of teacher educator identity discussed above. After discussing the educators' reflections, main themes related to identity are extracted and discussed. But before continuing, I present a second personal narrative.

PERSONAL NARRATIVE 2: STUDYING ABROAD
Immediately after tutoring linguistics for a year during my postgraduate honours qualification I secured a junior lecturer position in the same

department at Rhodes University. This involved conducting the same tutorials, but now included teaching a number of undergraduate courses in linguistics subjects, such as phonetics and phonology, and sociolinguistics. I continued this work for three semesters when I was fortunate enough to be awarded a scholarship to study for an MA in applied linguistics at Essex University in the UK. I discovered when I arrived at the university that second language teaching experience was required for entry to the programme, and, of course, I had none; having taught only linguistics to English 'first language' speakers at university level. I was by far the least experienced teacher in the rather large MA class, and I felt like a fraud! After completing the MA, I returned to South Africa with plans to become a high school teacher, and so enrolled in an accreditation-gaining higher education diploma, once again at Rhodes University. This one-year qualification got me thinking much more about teaching, and education more generally, and included two six-week stints teaching in high schools on a practicum experience. I also got my old job back as a part-time graduate tutor in the linguistics department for the year. However, after completing the diploma, in the mid-1980s, I felt uneasy about teaching in apartheid schools, and decided to pursue further study abroad. This time I was fortunate to receive a Fulbright Scholarship to study at Teachers College, Colombia University, towards my doctorate in TESOL. I arrived at the university to begin my studies, still without having taught an ESL or EFL class before! Within a few months I had a teaching job at a community college in New York City, where I taught a few hours a week for the next three years. At last, I started to feel like an English teacher. And at the same time, at Teachers College, I got a position as an adjunct instructor, which involved placing and then observing student teachers in city elementary and high schools. The observations were followed by one-on-one conversations about their teaching and we also held productive weekly seminars where we all got to share our experiences. So, in a small way, that was my entry into teacher education.

This narrative illustrates a somewhat tentative start towards becoming a language teacher educator. But it is probably true that for most teacher educators this journey is seldom smooth or predictable. Everyone's story is different. In my case, I was studying at the doctoral level, in TESOL, without having taught ESL before – although I did have classroom experience as a university graduate tutor and lecturer of linguistics. By the end of the doctorate I still had not taught English as a full-time teacher – although I had three years' experience working at a community college teaching English to adult immigrants for a few hours a week (incidentally, I also taught writing to ESL students hoping to gain entry to mainstream classes at the college). I observed student teachers on their practicum and commented on their teaching with very little experience myself, so could hardly call myself a teacher educator – although our approach was not to evaluate the teaching, but rather to describe and reflect on what happened and to consider and try out alternative practices (see Fanselow & Hiratsuka, 2019). My narrative signals my early developing identity as a language teacher educator. In particular, it shows the transition from teacher to teacher educator (see Williams, Ritter, & Bullock, 2012), albeit very hesitantly, since both identities had barely taken shape themselves. And because the narrative indicates my feelings of guilt, uncertainty, uneasiness, legitimacy, and accomplishment, it reveals the close interrelationship between identity and emotion (Gkonou & Miller, 2020). These and other dimensions of language teacher educator identity are explored in more detail in the reflections that follow.

## 2.1 Background to the Study

The doctoral programme in which the Colombian teacher educators are enrolled is an inter-institutional programme with a specialization in English language teaching education. The teacher educators are all very experienced English teachers, in schools or universities, and some have taught Spanish as well. A few have worked abroad for short periods of time, and all identify to varying degrees as teacher educators. What this means is that they have taught 'content' courses (e.g., linguistics, pedagogy, and sociolinguistics) to university students who intend to become English teachers, typically in pre-service teacher education programmes. They have also mentored student teachers during their practicum experiences and action research projects. Most have held some administrative or leadership positions in their institutions, such as course convener, programme coordinator, or head of department. At the time of the study, the teacher educators had varying levels of research experience, mainly classroom-based action research and projects attached to their previous qualifications, and some had carried out independent studies that were published in local journals. More recently, some have published conceptual pieces or research-based articles based on their doctoral work. Even so, all would probably described themselves as early career researchers (Murray & Male, 2005).

I had met some of the teachers before the study started through my participation in an annual conference in Colombia. At the same conferences I met and developed professional relationships with faculty at the university where the doctoral programme was located. So I was reasonably familiar with the regional, educational, and political context in which the study was carried out (Gómez-Vásquez & Guerrero Nieto, 2018; Pereira, Lopes, & Marta, 2015). The design of the study consisted of two narrative interviews with each participant four months apart. During narrative interviews (Chase, 2003) participants are invited to 'tell me about' (p. 88) their lived and imagined experiences, rather than being asked (only) direct questions, the aim being to elicit reflective stories co-constructed by both the narrator and the interviewer. Stories, as Kramp (2004) says, 'assist humans to make life experiences meaningful. Stories preserve our memories, prompt our reflections, connect us to our past and present, and assist us to envision our future' (p. 107), and are thus an ideal means for investigating the teacher educators' histories, desires, and ambitions.

The first interview was conducted at the end of the teacher educators' first year of study, and lasted about one hour. Topics covered included their personal biography, language learning and teaching history, work as a teacher educator, reasons for doctoral study, doctoral journey so far, and professional goals for the future. The second interview was slightly shorter and addressed a number of common themes that I had discovered after analyzing the first set of interviews. In what follows, the teacher educators reflect on their identities as language teacher educators in response to a direct question towards the end of the first interview that requested them to do so. I briefly discuss their responses to illustrate some of the features of the published definitions of teacher educator given above, the purpose being to 'bring them to life' with real personal experiences, and also to unpack them in finer detail, particularly as they pertain to *language* teacher educators. Before each interview excerpt I provide a short biography to introduce the teacher educator.

### 2.1.1 Ana

Ana grew up in a large city and struggled to learn English when at school. She decided nevertheless to 'study English teaching' at university and struggled there too. However, after extra lessons and with determined effort she began to make progress, to the extent that she started teaching English at an institute in the city while still an undergraduate. After graduation she worked in an elementary school, then decided to teach Spanish in Asia for a few months before returning to Colombia to complete a Master's degree while continuing to teach in numerous institutions. She got involved in teacher education during this time, supervising student teachers' action research projects. Ana desires a full-time position as a teacher educator at a university, but a lack of research experience (and publications) is preventing her from achieving this professional goal. Reflecting on her identity as a teacher educator she says:

1  it's so confusing
2  it's so confusing for different reasons
3  I want to see myself contributing to language teacher education from a decolonial perspective
4  meaning having a knowledge of our own
5  preparing our own materials
6  experiencing experiencing language teaching from our sense
7  I don't know if I will be able to do it
8  because this doesn't only depend on me
9  in the sense that I can contribute to teachers' education working at universities
10  but that depends if I will be accepted
11  if there is a position for me at local universities
12  because we also depend on economics
13  I came to the realization that because of studying this PhD
14  it doesn't mean that I'm going to be better received
15  because sometimes we think that
16  because of being educated
17  then that's going to grant us something
18  and that's not always the case because of economic reasons
19  I would like it to be like that
20  I would like to work preparing teachers to become teachers
21  and becoming a solid teacher educator right
22  yeah a teacher educator that has a discourse of her own.

Four aspects of Ana's teacher educator identity emerge from this reflection. The first (lines 1–2) is its complexity. She acknowledges that there is no straight answer when asked about her teacher educator identity; instead, being a teacher educator is 'confusing for different reasons'. Part of the confusion relates to two other identity aspects. Both are desires she has for the future. The first is her developing commitment to 'language teacher education from a decolonial perspective' (line 3), where her student teachers will have a 'knowledge of our own' (line 4) and prepare 'our own materials' (line 5). To achieve this, she faces a dilemma, however, and that is finding 'a position for me at local universities' (line 11). Here, as she articulates elsewhere in the interview, she is referring to a full-time academic position as a teacher educator with research responsibilities. She believes that occupying such an institutional position will enable her to become 'a solid teacher educator' (line 21), perhaps reflecting her image of an 'ideal' teacher educator, where she could practice 'a discourse of her own' (line 22), that is, enact a decolonial teacher education pedagogy (Domínguez, 2019). The problem is, however, for 'economic reasons' (lines 12 and 18) such a position might not become available. Even if it did, and even armed with her PhD, Ana commented that 'it doesn't mean that I'm going to be better received' (line 14). The fourth aspect of her teacher educator identity, then, interconnects with the macro context – this time economic – current in Colombia at the time.

*Identity keywords*: complexity of teacher education; decolonial pedagogy; university teacher educator; macro (economic) context.

### 2.1.2 Juan

Juan started learning English when he was ten years old. He attended a public school in a large city and, after a false start studying towards a science-oriented degree at university, he switched to English so as to become an English teacher. He majored in English and Spanish, and after completing his BA and Master's degrees he became a Spanish teacher for a year or so at a high school. Because of his advanced English proficiency he was asked to teach English. He then moved to a teaching position at university where he also became involved in English teacher education. Juan has been teaching for about fifteen years.

1  I am a person who is interested in the students
2  I want them to learn what is the implication of being a teacher
3  it doesn't matter the subject that I am teaching
4  but I really want them to learn what is the implication
5  what implies
6  because I think or I feel that our students nowadays
7  here in Colombia
8  they are starting doing the majors just without understanding what they are studying
9  and it really concerns
10 it is a really okay
11 it really worries me
12 because they are going to be teachers
13 and they are going to replicate those feelings in other people
14 so one of the things that I want to do
15 is that they understand what is to be a teacher
16 what they have to do
17 what they have to be as teachers
18 and other thing that can describe myself as a teacher is that

19  although I feel I could sometimes show myself as a severe teacher
20  very strict
21  but I'm not that way
22  and they feel sometimes that I am very demanding with them
23  but I am demanding
24  but I really care about them
25  if they have problems
26  if they have something
27  I really care
28  I understand and I listen to them right

Juan reveals two major dimensions of his teacher educator identity in his narrative. The first is his attitude towards his student teachers – undergraduate pre-service teachers of English in Colombia. He starts in line 1 by saying that he is 'interested in the students', and later repeats 'I really care about them' (lines 24 and 27). He adds, 'I understand and I listen to them' (line 28). These comments show Juan to be a teacher educator deeply committed to the welfare and advancement of his students (Kubanyiova, 2020). He may project an identity as 'a severe teacher' (line 19) who is 'very strict' (line 20) and 'very demanding' (line 22), but this is probably because he cares so much. And also because 'it really concerns' (line 9) and 'really worries' (line 11) him that his students are preparing to become teachers 'without understanding what they are studying' (line 8). In other words, he believes they do not know what it means 'to be a teacher' (line 15), or probably how to be an English teacher, and so they will be jeopardizing ('replicating', line 13) the learning of their future English students. His aim, instead, even if it means being somewhat 'demanding', is to get his student teachers to 'learn what is the implication of being a teacher' (line 2) – what they need to know and do in their future lives as practising teachers in Colombia.

*Identity keywords*: meaning of being a teacher; projected identity; caring teacher–teacher educator relationship; demanding work ethic.

### 2.1.3 Eduardo

Eduardo majored in a non-education field and worked in business for eight years where he acquired an interest in English because of the international work he was doing. He decided to take English classes at an institution in the large city where he lives. He then made a life-changing decision to return to university to complete another undergraduate degree majoring in English. He went on to do his Master's and has been an English teacher and teacher educator for twenty years.

1  I am a teacher educator who wants to share with the students
2  not for showing off
3  but for teaching actually teaching is that right
4  teaching is not have that specific perspective that teachers are over students
5  and students they have to look up to the teacher
6  just because he is always higher
7  no it's because
8  and I don't want my students to admire me actually
9  I just want them to see that I have a role
10  that I really have
11  I don't know if that is the correct word
12  I have influence in the way they see their profession
13  is more than that
14  I am also a person who is really demanding
15  and my students know about that
16  because they usually say that to me
17  they say 'teacher you're very kind
18  you're really friendly but you are really demanding'
19  possibly that's the way I have learned to do the things
20  and to me that is the way to get the things
21  and I just want to like pass that specific perspective on to my students
22  that they also see that hard work themselves

Eduardo shares some identity features with Juan. For example, he says that his student teachers perceive him to be 'really demanding' (lines 14 and 18), even though they refer to him as 'very kind' (line 17) and 'really friendly' (line 18). What Eduardo means is that he requires a strong work ethic from his student teachers. Working hard is the way he himself 'has learned to do the things' (line 19), 'to get the things' (line 20), and he wants to 'pass that specific perspective on to my students' (line 21). Eduardo desires to project a role model identity as a teacher educator (Lunenberg, Korthagen, & Swennen, 2007), not that he wants his students 'to admire me actually' (line 8) or to 'look up to' (line 5) him in a more powerful, 'higher' position. Instead, he wishes to 'share with the students' (line 1) the meaning of hard work and to 'influence in the way they see their profession' (line 12). Like Juan, he wants his student teachers to understand what it is they are getting themselves into by becoming English teachers, and to make the most from their teacher preparation experience through hard work and awareness.

*Identity keywords*: teacher educator as role model; demanding work ethic; projected identity; meaning of being a teacher.

### 2.1.4 Alex

Alex lives and works in a large Colombian city. He went to school there, and only started learning English 'seriously' when he went to university. He hadn't planned on becoming an English teacher, but dreamed of travelling and living in the United States. After graduation he taught English at a private English institute that catered for a wide variety of English learners. He completed his Master's five years later and progressively became involved in working with future teachers of English at the institute, and then at university. He describes himself as a language teacher educator as follows:

1  very dynamic very dynamic
2  resourceful
3  I would say that I have reached the level of teaching with example
4  why
5  specially at the Master's programme
6  with the different English teachers that I have worked with
7  is not only theory
8  all that they read for the module is applied by the teacher
9  by the person who is in front
10  I consider that the language teacher educator I am today
11  although I have some fails
12  I need to continue improving
13  I consider that first of all
14  I don't focus on the theory
15  I focus on the reflection about the theory
16  and the application of the theory in the teaching of my students
17  as a researcher that is something in which I admit I don't have much experience
18  as a researcher
19  although I have oriented different research projects at the Master's programmes and the BA programmes
20  I consider that I need to improve a lot
21  I feel I think I am a better language teacher educator than a researcher

Alex describes his teacher educator self as 'very dynamic' (line 1) and having 'reached the level of teaching with example' (line 3), meaning, like Eduardo, that he is role model to the English teachers in the Master's programme in which he works. Despite this level of perceived self-efficacy, Alex concedes that he has 'some fails' (line 11) and needs 'to improve a lot' (line 20). This need for further development is a common characteristic of teacher educators (Malm, 2020), and in Alex's case stems from a desire 'to continue improving' (line 12) and to foster meaningful learning in his student teachers, as we also saw with Juan. Alex believes his strength lies in his pedagogy, which 'is not only theory' (line 7) but emphasizes 'reflection about the theory' (line 15), and particularly 'the application of the theory in the teaching of my students' (line 16). His pedagogical approach makes connections between theory and practice and thus strives to be applicable to 'the person who is in front' (line 9). One domain in which Alex does not have much experience is 'as a researcher' (line 18), even though he has supervised ('oriented', line 19) 'research projects at the Master's programmes and BA programmes' (line 19). Again, he concedes that this is an area in which he needs to improve (line 20), and ends his reflection by saying that he feels he is a 'better language teacher educator than a researcher' (line 21), distinguishing a researcher identity from a superordinate teacher educator identity, to which he appears to give a pedagogical focus.

*Identity keywords*: teacher educator as role model; continuing professional development; application of theory; mentor of student teacher research; teacher educator as researcher.

## 2.1.5 Diego

Diego has been teaching for close to fifteen years. He was a product of the public school system in a large Colombian city, so when he started university to major in English and Spanish he 'actually didn't speak much [English], I didn't speak at all, probably'. Nevertheless, he started teaching English at a private institute before graduating, and then post-graduation he taught at a number of universities before embarking on a Master's in applied linguistics three years later. When he finished, he secured his current position at a university where the main focus is the preparation of future English language teachers.

1  I think I am a politically biased language educator
2  I think I am conscious of a political role
3  and I usually put it on the table
4  like I try to
5  I don't know to what extent students are expecting
6  but I try to make sure that every linguistic topic and every topic of a unit
7  which we're covering in a course
8  has space for reflection about society
9  has space for reflection about what is beyond the individual game
10  like meaningfully
11  definitely these students that we're working with will have

12  will be privileged because they will be needed
13  the prestige that the university already has
14  they will get a job definitely
15  many of our students
16  even before graduating
17  are already working as junior teachers
18  or teachers for children within the [name of] centre
19  so then what I'm having them do
20  is like offering them situations or contexts for reflection
21  about to what extent their profession is not going to be about their individual game
22  about you know like is going to be profitable for them
23  but what is going to happen with society
24  and like the role that they also have in probably recognizing what biases a society has

When articulating his teacher educator identity in his reflection, Diego reveals an emotionally reinforced social justice orientation (Boylan & Woolsey, 2015). He makes it clear that he approaches his work as 'a politically biased language educator' (line 1) and that he is 'conscious of a political role' (line 2) in what he does. He strives to ensure that this aspect of his identity-in-practice is visible to his students, to 'put it on the table' (line 3). In his pedagogy he gets his student teachers to shift their attention 'beyond the individual game' (line 9) by making 'space for reflection about society' (line 8). Diego teaches at an institution with 'prestige' (line 13), which means graduating teachers 'will be privileged' (line 12) and 'will get a job definitely' (line 14), and therefore life 'is going to be profitable for them' (line 22). He feels, therefore, that they need not be concerned about their own personal circumstances or about securing employment; in fact, some 'are already working as junior teachers' (line 17). Instead, Diego offers them 'situations or contexts for reflection' (line 20; see Johnson and Golombek (2020), who propose that language teacher education pedagogy be 'located' in sociocultural contexts, which will be discussed later in Section 3). In all aspects of the course, in 'every linguistic topic and every topic of a unit' (line 6), Diego encourages his students to reflect about society, and 'what is going to happen with society' (line 23). Perhaps most important for him as a teacher educator is for his students to consider 'the role that they also have in probably recognizing what biases a society has' (line 24). He is thus not only providing opportunities for his students to think about society beyond their immediate personal concerns, but to understand and question the ideologies they find there.

*Identity keywords*: social justice pedagogical orientation; political identity; macro sociocultural context.

### 2.1.6 Jenny

Jenny has been teaching English for about twenty-five years. She went to university with the intention of becoming an English teacher, and after completing her degree acquired her first job teaching English for specific purposes at a university. She has also taught at elementary school level, and has spent time abroad – several months in the United Kingdom as a Spanish teacher. After obtaining her Master's in applied linguistics fifteen years ago, she worked full-time at a university training pre-service English teachers.

1  well I am very committed with my job
2  I always think that we have to be a model for the students
3  what do I mean by model
4  that we have to be punctual
5  I have to show them that I prepared my classes right
6  I have to show them that I care for the students
7  because if I want them to be like that
8  if I want the students to be context sensitive I have to do the same right
9  so I think I should be a model for them
10  and at the same time I have to be able
11  not only to teach them a lot of methodology or theories
12  but to be aware of what they really are going to deal with
13  and that is something that has been challenging
14  because the students come with these questions every day
15  'what can I do with this'
16  some of the students
17  'what can I do with these situations'
18  and it makes me feel that as a language teacher educator I have to be updated
19  because probably when I was teaching
20  when I was a language teacher when I was working with these kids
21  when I was working at this institute I told you about
22  the situations I faced are very different from the situations my students are facing at the moment
23  so it means that I have to be updated
24  sometimes I feel that what I teach them
25  or tell them from my experience
26  is not useful for them

27  because the context that they're facing now is very different from the one
    that I faced
28  so I think we as language teacher educators have to be updated
29  and we have to be models

To demonstrate that she is 'very committed with my job' (line 1), Jenny desires
to be a role model for her student teachers (line 2). She does this in practical ways,
such as being punctual (line 4) and being prepared for her classes (line 5). But she
also wants her students 'to be context sensitive' (line 8), and so as a role model
believes that 'I have to do the same' (line 8). First, by context sensitive, and like
Diego, she aims to make her student teachers 'aware of what they really are going
to deal with' (line 12); that is, how they will operate as teachers in their future
sociocultural contexts. Even now, the students come to her with specific questions, such as 'what can I do with these situations' (line 17). Second, in order to
achieve this aim, Jenny needs to be current herself (see Hacker, 2008; Loughran,
2014) about these contextual conditions ('I have to be updated', line 18). She
repeats this belief in line 23, 'it means that I have to be updated', explaining that
when she worked in her previous job 'at this institute' (line 21), the 'situations
I faced' as an English teacher 'are very different from the situations' (line 22) her
students will face when they become English teachers. When she draws on her
early experiences to teach her current students, she feels that it is potentially 'not
useful for them' (line 26). This reinforces her belief that 'we as language teacher
educators have to be updated' (line 28).

*Identity keywords*: teacher educator as role model; continuing professional
development; being current; meaning of being a teacher; sociocultural context.

### 2.1.7 Yvonne

Yvonne grew up in a small city and learned English in the public school system.
She went on to major in English at university and, after graduating, started
teaching English at a private school, then later English for specific purposes at
university. While continuing to teach English she started to teach a 'course on
didactics' and later became more fully involved in formal teacher education,
including mentoring student teachers during their practicum. She obtained her
Master's degree and now works full time at a university in a large city.
Altogether Yvonne has been teaching for over twenty years.

1  as a dynamic teacher educator working with student teachers
2  pushing them
3  and achieving their personal and academic goals
4  I love dialoguing with them

5   so I think that is what I mean
6   what I have been doing but also what I would like to do
7   to keep working on my areas of interest
8   so when I work with my student teachers now
9   I try to interconnect at all times those agendas
10  and how to balance our practices
11  so I think that being a researcher is a wonderful way to learn more about my profession
12  to learn more about me
13  and to learn more about what I'm able to do as a teacher educator
14  so it is like a journey a path
15  and making connections with other teachers interested in the same area I am working on
16  in Latin America I think that we have a tendency to believe that Eurocentric thought is the only one we should consider
17  but I know that there are other wonderful experiences in Latin America
18  and I think it would be quite interesting for me to be in contact with them
19  to share what we're doing here
20  to give me the possibility to learn more about how they do it there
21  what decisions to make

Yvonne describes herself as a 'dynamic teacher educator' (line 1), meaning that when 'working with student teachers' (line 1) she actively gets involved 'dialoguing with them' (line 4) and 'pushing them' (line 2) to achieve their goals (line 3). As a teacher educator she has her student teachers' best interests at heart. Talking and listening to them is her pedagogical approach, something she 'loves' to do (line 4) and something she would like to continue doing (line 6) in the future. Having a dynamic teacher educator identity also means that Yvonne is willing and open to change, in her words 'to learn more' (line 11). This is a phrase she repeats three more times in her reflection (lines 12, 13, and 20). The first time, she references 'being a researcher' (line 11) and how doing so will enable her to 'learn more about my profession' (line 11). A researcher identity, as we saw with Alex, is considered to be an important facet of a language teacher educator identity, and Yvonne recognizes this. She also knows that by engaging in research she will 'learn more about me' (line 12) and 'what I'm able to do as a teacher educator' (line 13). Here she turns the focus onto her own development and her professional learning about teacher education. Her third mention of learning more (line 20) relates to her 'making connections' (line 15) with other teacher educators in Latin America who are 'interested in the same areas I am working on' (line 15). Yvonne thus desires to become part of a community of teacher educator scholars (Hökkä, Vähäsantanen, & Mahlakaarto, 2017) who, as Ana articulated in her reflection above, feel that a decolonial pedagogy and research focus would push them to question their 'tendency to believe that Eurocentric thought is the only one we should consider' (line 16). In this community, they could share ideas (line 19) about what they are doing, thus informing their practice ('what decisions to make', line 21).

*Identity keywords*: dynamic teacher educator; continuing professional development; macro sociocultural context; decolonial pedagogy; teacher educator as researcher; being part of a community.

## 2.2 Key Identity Themes in the Teacher Educator Reflections

The five published definitions of teacher educator discussed in Section 1.3 raised a number of broad ideas about who teacher educators are and what they do. Briefly, they can be summarized as follows:

1  Teacher educators work to support the professional learning of teachers.
2  Support could be in the form of coaching, training, mentoring, or formal academic instruction.
3  The teachers could be at various stages of their careers, from pre-service, to novice and early career, to in-service.
4  Teacher educators are teachers and scholars, and are typically active in research.
5  Teacher educators' practices usually occur within or are affiliated to institutional contexts.

The teacher educators' reflections in Section 2.1 reveal much more detail about these broad ideas – unpacking them to uncover finer meanings, and to understand their substance in real-life experience. It is also important to remember that the seven teacher educators are working in a context where they have been or still are English teachers, and where their student teachers are or will be teachers of English. So what we are hearing about are the reflections of *language* teacher educators. The finer details or key identity themes based on the reflections of the teacher educators are summarized in Table 1.

Although not a strict thematic analysis, I would propose that five main identity-related categories result from further examination of the key themes presented in Table 1; that is, by looking for similarities and patterns of association among them. I conclude this section with a brief description of the categories, which will be re-organized and refined by the end of the next section (Section 3).

**Table 1** Key identity themes from teacher educators' reflections.

| Key Identity Theme | Teacher Educator | Identity Descriptions |
|---|---|---|
| Complexity of teacher education | Ana | The complex nature of language teacher education, in which teacher educators experience their professional lives and construct their identities. |
| Decolonial pedagogy | Ana Yvonne | An approach to pedagogy in language teacher education that rejects Eurocentric or Anglo-Western theories, methods, and materials in (English) language teaching and research; reflected in the identity of teacher educators who take this stance. |
| University teacher educator | Ana | A teacher educator who holds a full-time position in a university, usually with research responsibilities (see teacher educator Types 3 and 4 in Section 1.2). |
| Macro (economic or sociocultural) context | Ana Diego Jenny Yvonne | The broader historical, sociocultural, economic, political, and institutional contexts with which the processes of language teacher education interconnect, and in which teacher educators negotiate and construct their identities. |
| Meaning of being a teacher | Juan Eduardo Jenny | The ongoing understanding that language teachers have of being or becoming a language teacher; teacher educators fostering this understanding as part of their identity-in-practice. |
| Projected identity | Juan Eduardo | The identities teacher educators project to their student teachers and colleagues as they go about their teacher education work; the public representation of their outer teacher educator self. |
| Caring teacher–teacher educator relationship | Juan | As integral to their practice and identity, teacher educators caring for their student teachers, promoting their well-being, and encouraging their personal, academic, and professional advancement. |

**Table 1** (cont.)

| Key Identity Theme | Teacher Educator | Identity Descriptions |
|---|---|---|
| Demanding work ethic | Juan Eduardo Yvonne | Through modelling or training, informing student teachers about the meaning and benefits of hard work; teaching them to practise this work ethic in their future teacher lives. |
| Teacher educator as role model | Eduardo Alex Jenny | Teacher educators being a role model for student teachers in terms of pedagogy and professional conduct. |
| Continuing professional development | Alex Jenny Yvonne | A commitment to continue learning as a teacher educator, to improve, to grow, and develop personally and professionally. |
| Application of theory | Alex | In teacher education pedagogy to focus not only on teaching theory but on how to apply theory in practice in the process of teaching; to apply theory in the classroom. |
| Mentor of student teacher research | Alex | Mentoring or supervising student teachers who undertake research projects as part of their formal studies; teacher educators identifying as a mentor of research. |
| Teacher educator as researcher | Alex Yvonne | Engagement with and in research for professional development, as an academic scholar or because of institutional requirements; identifying more or less as a researcher. |
| Social justice pedagogical orientation | Diego | Displaying and practising a moral and political stance in teacher education; promoting a social justice orientation in the teacher learning of student teachers. |
| Political identity | Diego | Being political and projecting a political teacher educator identity in all aspects of teacher educator work; in the classroom, the institution, and beyond. |

**Table 1** (cont.)

| Key Identity Theme | Teacher Educator | Identity Descriptions |
|---|---|---|
| Being current | Jenny | Constantly striving to achieve currency, to be up to date with relevant theories, methods, and policies; for the purposes of teacher educator knowledge and student teacher learning. |
| Dynamic teacher educator | Alex Yvonne | Teacher educators changing and developing, and remaining open and willing to change; to reflect on practice and try alternative practices. |
| Being part of a community | Yvonne | Sharing ideas and pedagogical experiences and practices with professional colleagues, and learning from them; seeking research collaborations. |

1 *Pedagogy*: language teacher education pedagogy refers to 'what teacher educators do and say in their activities and interactions and the reasoning behind those activities and interactions' (Johnson & Golombek, 2020, p. 117). This includes what they do with student teachers inside formal teacher education classrooms, as well as with teachers (one-on-one or in groups) outside of classrooms in schools or other settings where languages are taught. Teacher educator identities are enacted and constructed in the process of doing teacher education work (Barkhuizen, 2019a).

2 *Research*: teacher educator research refers to the research activity they engage in, which can vary according to level of desire and commitment, and whether teacher educators see research as part of their job description and their identity. Sometimes it may be institutionally required. Teacher educators have differing beliefs about the value of research for their professional learning (Amott & Ang, 2020), and differing conceptions of what research is or should be (Barkhuizen, 2020a), and thus identify as researchers to varying extents.

3 *Currency and development*: keeping constantly current and professional development (Hayes, 2019) often go hand in hand, because being up to date with theory, methods, and policy means enhanced self-efficacy and

feeling better able to support student teachers (Hacker, 2008). Currency and development relate to both pedagogy and research.

4 *Context*: this potentially ambiguous and variously interpreted concept (Douglas Fir Group, 2016) extends from micro levels, such as one-on-one mentoring partnerships and classrooms, to broader institutional and community levels, to even more macro levels such as geopolitical regions (nations) and beyond, for example international professional associations and global trends and events. Language teacher educators are embedded and active within those ever-changing spaces.

5 *Political and moral stance*: the fifth theme to emerge from the language teacher educator reflections has to do with the moral (Farrell, Baurain, & Lewis, 2020; Vanassche & Kelchtermans, 2016) and political (see Peercy et al., 2019) positions teacher educators take in the work they do. These positions are enacted in their pedagogical practices and in their research activity, and are integral to the identities they claim and project.

## 3 What Do Language Teacher Educators Do?

This section looks more closely at what language teacher educators do, and how what they do intersects with their teacher educator identities. To set the scene, I start with an overview of the process of becoming a new language teacher educator, highlighting particularly the potential identity tensions educators experience during this period of transition. To address the broad question of what teacher educators do, I use the eight propositions that Johnson and Golombek (2020) suggest constitute language teacher education pedagogy as a central domain for the knowledge-base of teacher education, and do so from the teacher educators' perspective, focussing particularly on their identity construction. To illustrate the propositions, I draw on concepts from a study by Hacker (2008) that explored the *learning* of language teacher educators. I conclude Section 3 by producing a language teacher educator identity conceptual framework that includes discussion of aspects less frequently examined in the literature.

## 3.1 Becoming a Language Teacher Educator

The picture often painted of language teachers transitioning to the role of language teacher educator is one of moving (in a linear fashion) from a position of relative comfort, confidence, and feelings of self-efficacy to a position where suddenly everything is unstable, unfamiliar, and problematic. Murray and Male (2005), for example, found in their study of new teacher educators in higher education contexts in the United Kingdom that:

One of the major challenges for the teacher educators in this study was to identify how they could draw on their accumulated professional knowledge and understanding of school teaching to achieve feelings of personal confidence and competence about inducting student teachers into the profession. (p. 136)

It may well be the case that teachers entering a professional or academic teacher educator position are confident in their subject matter and pedagogical knowledge, and may have considerable experience teaching language, but this is not the same for all teachers. Some may have had limited or inappropriate language teaching experience, or none at all, for example, taking on a teacher education role directly after completing a qualification (and which usually applies to those who perform well in that qualification). A further example peculiar to language teachers, and possibly even more so to English teachers, is that their work might have taken them to multiple countries to take up a mixture of full-time and part-time employment in all sorts of language learning institutions. This differs somewhat from the comparatively stable situation of teaching in a public school for ten to fifteen years, and then taking the path of gaining a further qualification, and subsequently moving on to a language teacher educator position in higher education, which might be more typical in the general education field. In sum, Goodwin et al. (2014) say, 'too many academics who may be hired to do teacher education work are not necessarily prepared, qualified, or even choose to do this work' (p. 298). Whether prepared or not, confident or not, experienced or not, the transition to being a language teacher educator is nevertheless a change in direction, and this means a disruption to the professional identity of the new teacher educator.

Various metaphors have been used to describe the move from teacher to teacher educator, including being on a journey, a career path, or even 'a rocky road' (Wood & Borg, 2010, p. 17), indicating that the transition may not always be a smooth one. Trent (2013) uses the concepts of boundaries and boundary-crossing to explore the transition with a group of teacher educators in Hong Kong. The crossings, says Trent, 'not only represent opportunities for learning but are also potentially conflictual, marginalizing experiences' (p. 262). Williams (2014) talks of entering a third space 'where activity systems of schools and universities intersect and overlap' (p. 316). Williams cites Zeichner (2010), who describes what he calls hybrid spaces as those that 'involve a rejection of binaries such as practitioner and academic knowledge and theory and practice, and involve the integration of what are often seen as competing discourses in new ways – an either/or perspective is transformed into a both/also point of view' (p. 316). It is within these spaces that for beginning teacher educators their former language teacher identity and new developing teacher educator identity begin to merge, or overlap, or re-shape in some form, as they learn new pedagogical practices, try to make sense of unfamiliar institutional norms and roles, work with different kinds of learners, and become researchers.

It is clear that two things will happen during the early stages of induction into becoming a teacher educator (and probably for much longer). One I have already mentioned – the former language teachers' identities will change. In Trent's (2013) study, the teacher educators' 'identities were shaped and reshaped in the transition' (p. 263); and in Murray and Male's (2005) study the teacher educators experienced 'significant adaptations to their previous identities as schoolteachers' (p. 126). The second thing that will happen, consequently, is that new teacher educators will experience some identity-related tensions in their professional life. Williams, Ritter, and Bullock (2012) actually use the word 'tensions' (p. 251); they add that these tensions may create a 'challenge' and a 'dilemma' (p. 250) for the teacher educators. Trent (2013) calls the identity boundary-crossing 'problematic' (p. 263) for the teacher educators, and Yazan (2018) says that they may 'feel professionally uncomfortable' (p. 144). Murray and Male (2005) use 'conflicts' (p. 139) to describe the clash of identities. One reason frequently cited in the research literature for conflict is articulated by Williams, Ritter, and Bullock (2012): 'Maintaining a teacher identity is very important because many beginning teacher educators perceive this as part of their professional creditability in the eyes of pre-service teachers and mentor teachers in schools' (p. 248). So, on the one hand, teacher educators desire to hold on to and make salient their teacher identity for the sake of credibility – to show their student teachers and their colleagues that they know what they're doing because they have the relevant experience – but, on the other hand, they also need to demonstrate that they're part of the community of (academic) teacher educators who are teaching teachers – drawing on and constructing for themselves a different knowledge-base and doing research, for example. This 'grappling' with identity (Golombek, 2017) and negotiating 'identity dilemmas' (Nelson, 2017) is something that continues to some extent throughout one's career as a teacher educator. Davey (2013), for instance, says that being a teacher educator involves 'an ongoing negotiation or dialogue among one's past history and experiences, one's values and ideologies and one's current socio-cultural and politico-historical context' (p. 143).

Finally, experiencing tensions in the process of establishing a teacher educator identity is not something that should be treated lightly, by both teacher educators themselves and host teacher education institutions. And yet, not much is done in terms of systematic induction for new language teacher educators (Wright, 2010). This, of course, refers to teacher educators who leave, fully or partly, language learning schools to become teacher educators in institutions of higher education (see Types 1–9 in Section 1.2) – and not school-based teacher educators or those solely in mentoring roles. The former are very much left to get on with the job themselves, which they typically do, drawing richly on their language teaching experience and their apprenticeship observing (Lortie, 1975) their own teacher educators, and enduring the inevitable sink or swim phenomenon in most aspects of their work. Where professional development has been made available for teacher educators (though not specifically *language* teacher educators), Amott and Ang (2020, p. 4) indicate that it has been found to have four features: (a) learning communities, similar to communities of practice, in which new teacher educators share knowledge and skills with each other and with more experienced colleagues; (b) supportive relationships, such as being assigned a more experienced teacher educator as a mentor; (c) reflective activities, which may include opportunities to collaborate in narrative writing with other teacher educators (Mendieta & Barkhuizen, 2020), for example, or to engage in critical self-reflection (see Peercy & Sharkey, 2020); and (d) research, which has been discussed above, to refer to engaging with and in research for the purposes of professional development and to establish securely an institutional academic researcher identity. I end this section with a personal narrative that takes me from the end of my doctoral studies to high school, and then to my first formal language teacher educator position at university.

PERSONAL NARRATIVE 3: FROM UNIVERSITY TO HIGH SCHOOL TO UNIVERSITY

After completing my doctorate at Teachers College, Colombia University, I returned to South Africa to take up a job teaching English as a Second Language (ESL) at a high school. The school was situated in the far north-west region of the country on the edge of the Kalahari Desert, and the majority of the students were thus Setswana speaking, an indigenous African language. I initially signed up for two years but ended up staying for four altogether, such was the rewarding nature of the professional experience. The school encouraged innovative teaching, curriculum development, and assessment practices, in which I enthusiastically engaged. I also gained some early leadership experience by establishing and becoming head of an independent ESL department within the school's organizational structure. Over the same period, I published a few chapters from my doctoral dissertation. After leaving the school I headed back to my alma mater, Rhodes University, where I accepted an academic position in the linguistics department (I had been a student there and also a graduate tutor). This time my teaching included sociolinguistics and numerous applied linguistics courses; applied linguistics being an area that the department was eager to grow. I was heavily involved in a graduate programme called English Language Teaching (ELT), and in fact became Director of the programme, teaching a number of its courses; well, those courses that required an experienced English teacher to teach them (or one with recent teaching experience, who was interested in language teaching and language teacher education as an academic endeavour). And I was the one who most closely fitted that description. The programme was small when I started, perhaps five to eight students. I thoroughly enjoyed teaching them. I had loads of classroom teaching experience to draw on, with real materials – lesson plans, worksheets, tasks, assessments, syllabus documents – readily available. I felt absolutely genuine and convincing in my teacher educator role, and cannot recall experiencing any identity tensions. I received excellent teaching evaluations, and the programme started to grow. I was also in a very supportive institutional environment, with collaborative and friendly colleagues, who I suspect were rather pleased to see someone else, rather than them, doing the applied linguistics content. Within a few years the programme grew to around twenty to twenty-five students, and my personal research agenda developed rapidly, with a three-pronged focus on multilingual education, teacher education, and sociolinguistics. I truly was starting to feel like a language teacher educator.

## 3.2 Doing Language Teacher Educator Work

In this section, I discuss each of the eight interrelated propositions put forward by Johnson and Golombek (2020), which they believe constitute language teacher education pedagogy as a central domain for the knowledge-base for language teacher education (LTE). I do so from the perspective of the teacher educator, focussing specifically on what they mean in relation to their identity. I want to stress here that Johnson and Golombek's (2020) propositions represent only one view of the processes or pedagogy of language teacher education, and I am not saying that these propositions indicate what should be happening in teacher education programmes. They themselves make the point that *context* is important (see below): the context of teacher education and the context of language teaching. And I have made the point a number of times myself so far in this document that these situated educational processes differ substantially from context to context – sociocultural, historical, geopolitical. Nevertheless, the propositions incorporate *interaction, mediation,* and *development,* which in different configurations (and with different outcomes, which we do not always know about) are probably common to all varieties of language teacher education. And central to all of this, and this is my focus here, is the identity of the language teacher educator; how it is embodied, negotiated, enacted, constructed, and re-shaped.

The eight propositions have their foundation in a Vygotskian sociocultural theoretical perspective, and thus Johnson and Golombek envision that:

> the dialogic interactions that unfold in our LTE programs as the very external forms of social interaction and activities … will become internalized psychological tools for teacher thinking, enabling our teachers to construct and enact theoretically and pedagogically sound instructional practices for their students. (p. 118)

Teacher educators are the mediators in this process, as they 'orient to and enact intentional and systematic pedagogies' (p. 119) that support the professional development of the student teachers. It is the teacher educators who set up and engage in the interactions and activities with the student teachers; they are integrally immersed in what goes on with their teacher education. And so are their identities. Who they are as language teacher educators interconnects with the processes of teacher education. While this is going on, Johnson and Golombek emphasize the need for language teacher educators to recognize that:

> while we are engaged in the present, we must collaboratively and cooperatively acknowledge the past and imagine the future, all the while recognizing what we are doing as happening in an evolving, ever-changing and challenging system. (p. 119)

The temporal dimension evident in this statement brings to the fore the dynamic nature of teacher educator identities. Poststructuralist theories of identity (see Block, 2013; Norton, 2013) maintain that identities change, in short-term interactions with other people and material objects, and over time. In other words, in enacting an LTE pedagogy teacher educators' identities are constantly in flux, in the day-to-day classroom interactions with student teachers, as well as longer term over the course of their careers.

Before getting on to the eight propositions, I introduce Hacker's (2008) study, which examined the nature of language teacher educator learning; that is, the experience of learning to become a language teacher educator in the particular contexts in which they were working as language teacher educators. In discussing each of Johnson and Golombek's (2020) eight propositions I make reference to concepts from Hacker's study. Her narrative inquiry included fifteen participants, all experienced teacher educators working in institutions of higher education in New Zealand. Data for the inquiry consisted of narrative interviews and numerous follow-up conversations with the participants. Following a detailed thematic analysis of the interviews and the storied configuration of each of the individual educator's experiences, Hacker inductively developed a conceptual framework of language teacher educator learning, with its core being a number of learning dimensions. The most salient of these are *teachers*, *teaching*, *professional position*, and *currency*. These dimensions apply to the learning of teacher educators, but it is very easy to see how they can be usefully applied to examine their *identities*.

*Teachers* is the dimension concerned with language teacher educators' experiences 'relating to the people they teach or in some way assist to develop as promoters of language learning, and who are often referred to by the educators as their students' (Hacker, 2008, p. 140). Identities are negotiated and constructed in social interaction with others, and for teacher educators the teachers they work with are their main interactional focus. Their relationship primarily involves the dimension of *teaching*, which is concerned with language teacher educators' experiences 'relating to any aspect of their own teaching in their work as language teacher educators in their contexts of practice' (Hacker, 2008, p. 139).

The *professional position* dimension is concerned with language teacher educators' experiences relating to their particular formal job descriptions: 'This involves the activities and requirements that educators are recommended or expected to engage in, perform and meet in their professional positions in their contexts of practice' (Hacker, 2008, p. 139). Aligned with these positions are particular roles and responsibilities, and the positions are usually clearly visible to others in the workplace. By *currency* Hacker (2008) means language teacher educators' experiences relating to 'the most recent information available in the fields in which they have interests or responsibilities as language teacher educators' (p. 140). This may relate practically and/or theoretically to their pedagogy or research, or to other involvements they have in their capacity as language teacher educators, such as leaders or curriculum developers. Johnson and Golombek's (2020) eight propositions follow.

### 3.2.1 LTE Pedagogy Must Be Located

Teacher education takes place in the particular contexts where teacher educators do their work. And future language teachers will practise in particular contexts.

I have addressed 'context' a number of times already in this Element (see, for example, Section 2.2). My message has been, as Johnson and Golombek (2020) remind us, that 'context is not limited to specific geopolitical boundaries but includes socio-political, sociohistorical, and/or socioeconomic contexts that shape and are shaped by local and global events' (p. 120). What happens locally in language teacher education, therefore – in classrooms, in teaching practicums, in action research projects – is interconnected with much broader scales of context, larger ideological discourses with which teacher educators and student teachers engage. Teacher educators need to provide opportunities for teachers to reflect on and make sense of their development in the context of their teacher education, and also to provide them with the resources so that they can continue to locate their teaching in their particular working contexts when they start to teach. Teacher educators also need to reflect on and make sense of their own practices and continuing development in their working contexts, in relation to the past, the present, and the future.

In this relationship with context, both in the actual process of teacher education, in collaboratively imagining the future teaching of their student teachers, and in imagining their own future teacher education practices (including pedagogy and research), teacher educators negotiate and construct their identities. This broad proposition, that LTE pedagogy must be located, aligns with all four of Hacker's dimensions, possibly just like the other propositions do too. For example, the teacher educators' primary focus is the *teachers* they work with; this stems from the *professional position* they hold within their institution, a position with which they identify. In the process of *teaching*, teacher educators interact with teachers, form relationships with them, mentor them, and construct their own identities, as they locate the teachers' and their own ongoing development in context. To do so effectively requires *currency*, being and feeling up to date and knowledgeable in one's field. Teacher educator's identities are implicated in all aspects of this process – they relate to what they do with student teachers and how they do it, how they see themselves in practice and the effect they have, and how others see them.

### 3.2.2 LTE Pedagogy Must Recognize Who the Teacher Is and Who the Teacher Wishes to Become

This proposition aligns most closely with Hacker's *teachers* dimension; a concern, interest, and passion for the student teachers teacher educators work with. The proposition means that teacher educators must get to know 'who the teacher is and who that teacher wants to become' (Johnson & Golombek, 2020, p. 121). And it relates to teacher identity – giving the student teachers (or in-service teachers) the opportunity to try out and reflect on their developing identities; and to align those identities with their teaching practice. For this to happen requires a certain kind of teacher educator – one who sees the importance of self-reflection as a means of understanding both who one is and is becoming (one's identity) and one's teaching actions. When this happens teacher learners are 'active mediators of their own learning' (Farrell, 2018, p. 4). As teacher educators strive to get to know who their student teachers are, they also work to understand themselves. Teacher educators thus need to recognize who they are as language teacher educators and who they wish to become. In other words, this proposition also applies to teacher educators. In the *being* and *becoming* they self-reflect on their developing identities, in context, with the same goals as their student teachers; that is, to learn more about themselves, their teaching practices, their socio-cultural and working contexts, in order to develop and grow as people and teacher educators. Hacker's *teachers* dimension, with its emphasis on teacher educators *assisting student teachers to develop as promoters of language learning*, could be re-interpreted for teacher educators to mean assisting them to develop as promoters of learning to teach.

### 3.2.3 LTE Pedagogy Must Be Intentional and Goal-Directed: These Intentions and Goals Must Be Made Explicit

For LTE pedagogy to be intentional and goal-directed, teacher educators must 'make explicit their motives, intentions, goals, and ideologies when designing, sequencing, and enacting' teacher education pedagogy (Johnson & Golombek, 2020, p. 121). This really opens up teacher educators to scrutiny from their student teachers, and also their colleagues. People get to see what they do, and figure out why they do it that way. It exposes not only their practices, but also their ideas about language teaching and learning, about teacher education, and about education in general – ideas that are embedded in the teacher educators' personal and professional histories, and their political convictions. Following this proposition, teacher educators would, of course, attempt to make their intentions and goals explicit but there always remain unspoken, un-signalled (even hidden) aspects of one's practices in classroom interactional encounters. It is sometimes difficult to find a balance between being explicit and 'overexposure' where too much of oneself is revealed, thus leaving oneself vulnerable (Vanessche & Kelchtermans, 2016) or potentially crossing some ethical line. Identities could be contested by others, or by the teacher educators themselves. Hacker's *teaching* dimension – an educator's focus on pedagogy for language teachers – carries some risks, therefore.

### 3.2.4 LTE Pedagogy Must Create Opportunities to Externalize Everyday Concepts While Internalizing Relevant Academic Concepts Through Authentic, Goal-Directed Activities of Teaching

What this proposition means is that teacher educators need to work towards supporting student teachers to unite their everyday concepts – gained from experience and often implicit and unanalyzed – with the new academic concepts they encounter in the teacher education programme. The academic concepts are those generated by research and other scholarship (theorizing) in the field of language teaching and learning; they are the 'theory' in the complex theory–practice relationship. So the goal is to link the academic concepts to teaching practice so that teachers are better able to understand their teaching and thinking about teaching, and thus make more informed pedagogical decisions about future activity. For teacher educators, remaining current (Hacker's (2008) *currency* dimension) is vitally important. They too are concerned with uniting their everyday concepts, generated from previous language teaching experience, for example, but not systematically analyzed or reflected upon, with recent developments in the disciplines of language teaching and teacher education; for example, new knowledge about second language acquisition, multilingual education, online language learning. To keep in touch with the new knowledge requires teacher educators to strive for currency. One of the participants in Hacker's study, a senior manager of a teacher education programme, regularly attends Ministry of Education workshops; another insists on maintaining close and constant contact with language learners; and a third belonged to a supportive teacher educator learning community who worked in the same curriculum area as she did. These 'currency strategies' kept them up to date with what was happening in their fields and allowed them to internalize new concepts applicable to their teacher education work.

### 3.2.5 LTE Pedagogy Must Contain Structured Mediational Spaces Where Teachers are Encouraged to Play/Step Into Being and Becoming a Teacher

Hacker's (2008) *teaching* and *teachers* dimensions are most salient with regard to this proposition; in the process of creating mediational spaces for teachers, in which they take part in goal-directed activities and interactions, teacher educators become mediators, expert others, models, providers of emotional support, and instructors of academic concepts (Johnson & Golombek, 2020). Their focus is centrally on their teachers and also on their own teaching, so that they achieve the goal of promoting the development of their student teachers – to enable them to 'try out emerging teacher identities, alternative instructional practices, and new modes of engagement in teaching' (p. 123). Doing all of this is demanding 'identity work' (Miller, Morgan, & Medina, 2017). Teacher educators have to be vigilant of maintaining their mediator identity in their interactions with their student teachers, without overstepping their responsibilities, for instance, 'model' and 'the expert'. This identity juggling goes on in spaces beyond the teacher education classroom, in schools during the practicum, as supervisor of student research projects, and as leaders or coordinators of programmes. Mediational spaces should be safe for both teachers and teacher educators – safe for both to explore, try out, and question their identities collaboratively.

### 3.2.6 LTE Pedagogy Must Involve Expert Mediation That Is Responsive to Teachers' Immediate and Future Needs

This proposition emphasizes 'responsive mediation', whereby expert teacher educators first (see proposition three above) make explicit their goals, cognitions, and emotions in their interactions with their student teachers. In these interactions they aim to learn about and understand their teachers as much as possible (i.e., upping a notch their responsiveness to them); to 'fine-tune their understandings of teachers' immediate needs and capabilities, engaging in responsive mediation, as they attempt to identify the upper limits of teachers' potential' (Johnson & Golombek, 2020, p. 124). This requires even more attention from teacher educators to their teachers, the nature and effect of the interactions they engage in with them, and ultimately to their development. As if this is not demanding enough, at the same time teacher educators have to pay close attention to their own teaching, interactions, and learning. Once again, Hacker's *teachers* and *teaching* dimensions are crucially relevant here. From the perspective of teacher educators, responsive mediation is about focus, listening, being open, decision making, supporting, and feeling. This is taxing indeed. Identities are exposed in the process, which implies they are open to inspection and challenge. Further, as Johnson and Golombek point out, teacher educators are expected to perform other roles in institutions (Hacker's *professional position*, through which teacher educators learn to be teacher educators and in which they continually construct their teacher educator identities), such as evaluators of teaching performance or supervisors of research, and these types of 'ascribed' identities add further authority to their enacted expertise and perceived power. When teacher educators interact with their student teachers in these situations, they (co-)construct multiple identities – those they desire to project, those institutionally ascribed, and those recognized by the teachers – and this can lead to emotional tensions, such as vulnerability, disappointment, and anxiety, on the part of *both* student teachers and the teacher educators, which the latter will necessarily respond to and manage.

### 3.2.7 LTE Pedagogy Must Have a Self-Inquiry Dimension, Involving Teacher Educators and Teachers Working Together or By Themselves, In Which They Seek to Trace Teacher Professional Development As It Unfolds Over Time and Place

As student teachers do their teacher education work, whether that be activities with fellow student teachers and the teacher educator, or classroom teaching practice during practicums, they must, according to this proposition, engage in self-inquiry; that is, to reflect deeply on and ask questions about their ongoing development as teachers over time, in order to understand it and position it within their socio-cultural, institutional contexts of practice. Johnson and Golombek (2020) suggest that teacher educators mediate this process of self-inquiry, for example by working with the teachers to provide feedback, commentary, and support during the inquiry activities, and thus not always leaving the students to work on their own. Teacher-educator-mediated narrative inquiry is one approach to inquiry that allows the teachers to make meaning of their experiences through the stories they tell. Stories have a temporal dimension, and so teachers can trace their development over time – from the past and into their imagined and actual future teaching lives – and they also have place and people dimensions, where the action of stories unfolds with other characters in the story world (see Barkhuizen, 2020b). In the narrative space that these interrelated dimensions create, and mediated by teacher educators, student teachers self-inquire, become aware of, monitor, think about, and understand their development. All of this applies to the teacher educators as well. Because of their institutional *professional position* (Hacker, 2008) teacher educators are usually required to do research (see types of language teacher educators in Section 1.2), manifesting their researcher identity. Besides the goals of publishing and advancing their careers (and nurturing their academic identities), for teacher educators the aim of gaining further knowledge about and keeping up to date in their field (Hacker's *currency*) is part of their own professional development. Narrative inquiry is certainly an option for such self-inquiry purposes.

### 3.2.8 LTE Pedagogy Must Demonstrate a Relationship of Influence Between Teacher Professional Development (As a Result of LTE Pedagogies) and Student Learning

Pre-service and in-service teachers participate in language teacher education so that they can develop as language teachers; specifically, to learn how to teach and learn about teaching language to their students. A 'relationship of influence' (Johnson & Golombek, 2020, p. 125) refers to this connection to student learning. An important question to ask, therefore, is: how do the activities of teacher education – what teacher educators and student teachers do in their interactions together – influence the language learning of the teachers' students? In Hacker's (2008) explanation of her *teachers* dimension, she references the teacher educator's relating to their student teachers 'as promoters of language learning' (p. 140). In other words, their interest in and commitment to their teachers is undertaken with both insight and foresight; they are ultimately concerned about the language learning of people who are not present in the teacher education happening now. A relationship of influence might also refer to the influence that teacher educators have on their own student teachers. In a similar way to the *teacher educator–teacher–language learner* relationship there exists an institutionally oriented *teacher education programme–teacher education–teacher* relationship. In these two relationships of influence, the teacher educator has slightly different roles, and claims and exhibits different identities. Just like the former, the latter is worthy of further investigation (see Section 5). The question here is: how do the activities of teacher education programmes – what programmes offer and what teacher educators do – influence the teaching learning of the student teachers?

The above eight propositions obviously have a strong focus on pedagogy, since they are the 'central domain' for the knowledge-base of language teacher education (Johnson & Golombek, 2020, p. 119). They are also clearly founded on the principles of sociocultural theory. However, if one takes a look at the key identity themes that emerged from the reflections of the Colombian English teacher educators (see Table 1, Section 2.2), it is noticeable that many of them make an appearance in the discussion of the eight propositions in this section. So, although I hesitate to claim that the sociocultural theory-based propositions are universally applicable – that all teacher educators do or should operate in this way – I do believe that many of their characteristics would be evident in language teacher education programmes, activities, and processes in other contexts. This, again, is particularly from the perspective of pedagogy and also research (inquiry). Less is said about the other activities that teacher educators engage in, such as institutional service, taking on leadership positions, and professional and community involvement. The next section will look a little more closely at these teacher educator activities.

## 3.3 The Identity Work of Language Teacher Educators

It is probably true to say that ultimately language teacher educators are concerned about language learning. Most will have been language teachers at some time in the past and some even continue to be while working as teacher educators. Most would have learnt another language, if not more than one, and many may even be teaching teachers how to teach that language. Teacher educators' language learning histories are intimately entwined with the teacher education work they do; that is, they draw on their experiences of learning and using (and teaching) language (Varghese, 2017), and in the process construct identities that legitimize their professional work as well as who they are, for themselves and for their students and colleagues. The interest and often passion for languages and language learning – as well as their dedication to the development and well-being of their student teachers (Hacker, 2008) – are manifest in language teacher educators' commitment to language teacher education (Kani, 2014). This commitment is reflected in varying levels of 'active participation in a wide range of communities of practice' (McKeon & Harrison, 2010, p. 38), and it is within these interrelated and often competing communities that teacher educators' professional identities are continuously shaped and reshaped. Malm (2020) references teacher educators' roles as emerging from three major domains, which could easily be perceived as communities, with their distinct discourses and practices: teaching/pedagogy, research/scholarship, and administrative/service. One might assume that these three are applicable only to teacher educators in higher education institutions, specifically academic teacher educators. However, defining them more loosely, it could be argued that all language teacher educators, whatever type they are (see Section 1.2), engage in different forms of teaching, research (including self-inquiry), and administration or service. I describe these domains in more detail below, where I add a fourth: briefly, what I do is split the service domain into two, creating institutionally oriented service work and community service work external to the institution, such as working with professional associations and governmental organizations, for example. These four interrelated domains are represented in Figure 1.

Figure 1 represents four interrelated areas of language teacher educators' work; four communities within which teacher educators do their professional work and negotiate their professional teacher educator identities. Before describing it further, I acknowledge that the figure does not completely or precisely capture all the work of teacher educators, and also that it does not apply to all teacher educators in all contexts. However, I believe that it serves a useful purpose by illustrating the interconnectedness of the different aspects of teacher educators' work, the different roles they play, and therefore the multiple identities they negotiate, construct, draw on, and project in these different professional communities. The figure also emphasizes the centrality of the *language teacher educator* in the processes of teacher education, a position often neglected in the scholarly and research literature. And most important for our discussion here is that the *identity* of the teacher educator is also positioned in the centre of the diagram.

Just a brief note about the design of the figure. It contains four inter-linked outer circles, each representing the four domains or communities of teacher

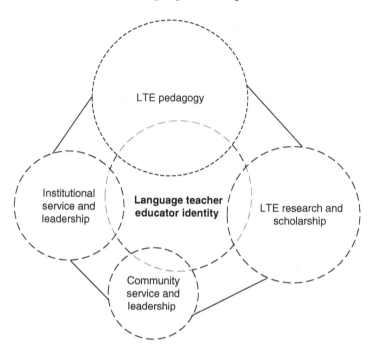

**Figure 1** The identity work of language teacher educators.

educator work. Their inter-relationship is shown by the straight lines that join them and also by their intersecting with the inner circle, which represents the teacher educator's identity. The four outer circles are of slightly different sizes, representing actual workload and 'identity-load' associated with those domains. This may be more or less true for one type of language teacher educator, typically those working in institutions of higher education. The size of some of the circles might expand or shrink (or even disappear) depending on the kind of teacher educator one is and the contexts in which they work.

A final point before describing the four domains. Being a member of four communities – performing roles and constructing related identities within these communities – inevitably means that 'struggle and conflict ... can arise from the interplay of discourse and agency' (Trent, 2013, p. 272), meaning that within and across communities (the four working domains) teacher educators' identities can be contested if what they do and say is perceived to be in non-alignment with the dominant discourses of that particular community. This is particularly the case with beginning teacher educators, who 'experience institutional political or power structures that challenge their sense of belonging' (Williams, Ritter, & Bullock, 2012, p. 250). As a result, in some cases teacher educators find themselves complying with institutional norms (see *conforming*, Section 5) even when they really do not agree with them or imagine themselves identifying with their related practices. Feelings of marginalization can result. This potentially applies to all four domains. This is not always the case, however. Teacher educators' practices and contributions may very well align with current community discourses and be acknowledged, accepted, and promoted. They may even transform the community in some ways. When this happens, teacher educators would identify closely with the community, aligning with it and experiencing a sense of belonging.

Having identities associated with and emerging from the four interrelated communities would inevitably mean that teacher educators experience some internal conflicts. How often do we hear academics say something like, 'I love teaching and research, but hate admin'? Consequently, they resent having to do administrative service when required to and seldom take on management or leadership roles within their institutions. They see their primary identity as teachers of teachers. Others do as well, and these, for example, might like to be more research active, but a heavy teaching load might prevent them from doing so. Their desired researcher identity is thus suppressed. And yet others may seek and thrive in institutional administrative roles, coordinating programmes and leading departments. And doing it well and making an essential contribution to the success of the community. The point here is that with these multiple roles and identities, the potential exists for tensions to arise when teacher educators try to balance their preferences, allegiances, and skills. In what follows, I provide brief descriptions of the four teacher education domains, paying particular attention to how they pertain to the work and identities of *language* teacher educators.

### 3.3.1 LTE Pedagogy

Much of what has been discussed so far in this Element, especially in Section 3.2 above (Johnson & Golombek's (2020) eight LTE pedagogy propositions), relates to pedagogy. This is because it is the core work of teacher educators, and thus represented by the largest of the four circles in Figure 1. Without in some way being involved in teacher education pedagogy – interacting with teachers about their professional development – one could hardly call oneself a teacher educator. In other words, all language teacher educators must do pedagogy, which will include some or all of the following:

- Teaching language or teaching about languages.
- Teaching language teaching methods, including the use of appropriate materials and assessments.

- Teaching 'content' subjects such as second language acquisition, sociolinguistics, discourse analysis, and academic literacy.
- Providing supplementary language support, particularly for speakers of languages other than the medium of teacher education.
- Mentoring student teachers during their internship or practicum experience.
- Observing practice teaching and mediating feedback.
- Mentoring student teachers' exploratory action research or narrative inquiry projects.
- Supervising graduate student research.

A language teacher educator's identity is fluid and constantly changing but whatever shape it takes at any particular time and place it will always include, often primarily, a pedagogical dimension. As members of an *LTE pedagogy* community, language teacher educators identify as teachers, mentors, and supervisors, and although this identity may fade at times or over time as they take on other roles, the core of who they are will always be a teacher.

### 3.3.2 LTE Research and Scholarship

This circle in Figure 1 is slightly smaller than the pedagogy circle for two reasons: (a) not all teacher educators are required by their institutional employment conditions to engage in research, and therefore don't, although all should be encouraged to do so or at least be involved in self-inquiry for the purposes of professional development (and be given time and support for this); and (b) even for those teacher educators who do research, it is usually to a lesser extent than their teaching responsibilities. The advantages of being research active have been discussed above (e.g., we saw good examples in the reflections of the Colombian teacher educators in Section 2.1), and include remaining current with ideas in the field (Hacker, 2008), learning more about one's own area of professional interest, making contact and collaborating with other scholars, and continuing to develop professionally. What does having a teacher educator researcher identity entail?

- Engaging in self-inquiry in the form of (exploratory) action research or narrative inquiry projects.
- Establishing and implementing a research programme, which could be up to half or more of a designated institutional workload.
- Carrying out research projects independently or in collaboration with colleagues on topics relevant to language teacher education or related fields.
- Disseminating research findings in publications and at conferences, workshops, and seminars, locally and internationally.

- Drawing on research findings to inform pedagogy and one's own professional development.
- Using findings to inform relevant curriculum and policy development at institutional level or macro levels of government.

Enacting a researcher identity in language teacher education certainly has its benefits, as pointed out above. In fact, doing exceedingly well as a researcher – publishing books and articles in high-profile journals, for example – can lead to a major identity shift, so that teacher educators begin to feel like and to be recognized primarily as researchers. Invitations to present at conferences and to contribute to books follow, and this reinforces the self-perceptions of a researcher identity. Identity dilemmas and feelings of resentment may result when these teacher educators are reminded by their institutions that they have pedagogical and service duties to fulfil. Similar feelings may emerge in teacher educators who conduct self-study or other self-reflective practices that are not recognized as rigorous research by their institutions (Cochran-Smith, 2005). In some institutions, simply being a teacher educator, whether doing research or not, is enough not to be taken seriously as an academic (Goodwin et al., 2014; Peercy et al., 2019).

### 3.3.3 Institutional Service and Leadership

There are always administrative and management tasks associated with teaching. As all teacher educators know, even running one course involves mundane tasks such as monitoring attendance, booking rooms and equipment, conducting course evaluations, and submitting grades. These may increase in volume and require extensive paperwork in more bureaucratic institutions or at times of organizational transformation. However, other service contributions can be more meaningful in the lives of teacher educators, and they could also potentially facilitate the smooth running of the institution beyond the teacher education classroom. The *institutional service and leadership* circle in Figure 1 is smaller than the pedagogy and research circles. For most teacher educators this reflects the amount of work time they spend as teacher educators. It is also probably true to say that it reflects how teacher educators perceive their professional identities. Very few would identify as an administrator, for example. Some of the service and leadership contributions language teacher educators typically make include the following:

- Administering courses, either in-classroom or online, which includes close liaison with student teachers and institutional administrators.
- Co-ordinating practicums, including placing student teachers in language schools, meeting and planning with co-operating teachers, and scheduling school visits.

- Co-ordinating programmes beyond the level of courses, such as a major (e.g., TESOL), a qualification (e.g., MA), certificate (e.g., CELTA), or an in-service teacher professional development programme (e.g., a series of workshops or a conference).
- Communicating with teacher accreditation bodies if student teachers are planning to work in educational systems that require official accreditation.
- Liaising with Ministries or Departments of Education to remain informed of syllabus, curriculum, and policy updates, and to contribute to discussions regarding these developments.
- Serving on committees at departmental, faculty, and university level, including chairing the committees when taking on leadership roles.
- Heading a department or school within an institution of higher education, which would involve responsibility for budget and staffing, as well as mentoring junior faculty, supporting all faculty, and leading by example.

As teacher educators advance in their careers they might move into management positions and take on leadership roles within programmes and higher up in institutions; their re-constructed identities would reflect these changes. For early career teacher educators, performing service and taking on leadership roles are important for the purposes of gaining tenure and promotion. Some of these teacher educators might resent having to do the service and consider it a necessary evil (disrupting their research activity, for example) to be tolerated as they work towards their career goals. In the process they might experience tensions or disempowerment as they acclimatize to the systems and requirements of their institutions (Murray & Male, 2005). Performing service does not necessarily lead to an institutionally imposed identity; some teacher educators might willingly seek opportunities to become engaged in administrative work or to take on leadership roles, seeing this aspect of their work as important to their professional development and to who they want to be as teacher educators, particularly outside the institution.

### 3.3.4 Community Service and Leadership

A recent publication by the British Council (2017) presents a framework for the continuing development of teacher educators, and lists as one of its recommended professional practices, 'promoting the teaching profession through examples of creativity, innovation, passion, and vision within teacher education and within teaching' (p. 16). This, of course, is achieved through interactions with student teachers in teacher education classrooms, mentoring relationships and research supervision, as well as through research activity and the dissemination of relevant and useful research findings. However, it is also achieved through professional activities outside of these domains, and outside the institution, for example through networking and sharing practices and expertise through forums, webinars, conferences, and short-term professional development programmes. Teacher educators can develop quite high-profile identities within these communities, especially if they become particularly active, or take on leadership roles, thereby modelling leadership in the profession (Smith, 2005); for example, serving as president of a language teaching association, or as editor of a regional language teacher education journal. Institutions may even offer release time for such activities, and would certainly consider them to be significant contributions in tenure and promotion applications. The following are just a few examples of the wide range of possible professional community service contributions teacher educators engage in:

- Participating in professional language teaching associations, perhaps serving on or chairing sub-committees or executive committees.
- Sitting on boards or advising community language schools for immigrant or refugee language learners, and preparing their language teachers.
- Participating in curriculum development at regional or national level.
- Contributing to the work of external language assessment or examining bodies.
- Conducting professional development workshops for language teachers in local schools.
- Organizing and presenting at language teacher conferences.
- Securing funding for collaborative research projects involving student teachers and teachers.
- Participating in language-in-education planning at regional and national level.
- Examining PhD and MA theses and dissertations from other universities in the field of teacher education.
- Serving on teacher education journal editorial boards and reviewing article submissions.
- Engaging with Ministries or Departments of Education to seek opportunities to gain and develop 'knowledge of current local or government initiatives' (Amott & Ang, 2020, p. 5).

The *community service and leadership* circle is the smallest of the four circles in Figure 1. This is because language teacher educators probably identify least with this community domain. I say 'probably' because first and foremost their official job description places them within an institution with an assigned *professional position* (Hacker, 2008). For most teacher educators this is where their key responsibilities lie, where their student teachers are, and where the work they do gets remunerated. It is possible not to do professional community service. On the other hand, there are some teacher educators who are heavily committed to community service and leadership, and willingly so. It is something they desire to do; they perceive that work to be integral to who they are as teacher educators. This section concludes with a personal narrative, in which I reflect on some of my service and leadership contributions.

PERSONAL NARRATIVE 4: LEARNING ABOUT LEADERSHIP

I spent nearly ten years at Rhodes University in South Africa, building the graduate ELT teacher education programme and teaching applied linguistics courses. I also ensured I maintained contact with language teachers in schools through my research and other professional activities, including working for an independent national examinations board, where I set, graded, and moderated external examinations in the subject *English Second Language*. My next academic position took me to the University of Auckland in New Zealand. I joined a very active department with some high-profile researchers and very experienced teacher educators, and I felt inspired to be working with such colleagues. My first academic year saw me teaching on four courses with large classes of current and future language teachers from diverse local and international backgrounds. For a newcomer to the university, I also found generous support for my research, in terms of both funding and time. Within six months I was asked to be deputy head of the department and, within another year, head of department. I was still finding my own way around the large university (never mind trying to settle in a new country) and so took on these roles reluctantly. There was only a small reduction in my teaching workload and research expectations remained as high as ever. The department was thriving at the time, with good student numbers, reasonably happy faculty, comfortable facilities, and adequate funding available for teaching and research support. Tasks such as managing the budget, planning teaching schedules, and dealing with the endless requests and deadlines from administration was something I easily learned and often enjoyed doing. There was always someone to ask and always someone to help. The part of the role I looked forward to the most was working with my teacher educator colleagues. I had the opportunity to work with them more closely, not only in the classroom but also in conversations about their development, their future plans, their problems, their successes. I learned a lot about language teaching and teacher education from them – with their vast experience of working in countries around the world, teaching in a wide range of contexts, and researching in areas unfamiliar to me. During my nearly four years as head of department my professional identity was pushed and pulled in many different directions as, for example, I tried to emphasize my teacher educator identity in some situations but was positioned as manager by colleagues, as I positioned myself as researcher at certain times but was instead identified by the institution as leader. These tensions certainly caused some stress in my working life, but I always tried to learn from them. A few years later when the department merged with two other departments to form a large school (like they tend to do in modern universities), incorporating Asian and European languages, I became the inaugural head of that school. The tensions, identity struggles, and related emotions intensified of course, but doing that institutional service and leadership also had enormous personal benefits. It opened up spaces for interaction with new professional colleagues, it enabled new networks and travel, and it taught me about disciplinary areas with which I was less familiar. One also hopes that one's work and effort makes a contribution to one's colleagues' professional lives and to the institution as well.

## 4 Further Professional Development of Language Teacher Educators

Vanassche and Lelchtermans (2016) refer to teacher education professional development as a learning process that 'spans one's career' (p. 356). This professional development can take many different forms, such as self-inquiry, carrying out research, attending conferences, working with a mentor, and participating in workshops and seminars. It can also involve further formal study, including enrolling in Master's and doctoral qualifications. When teacher educators embark on in-service graduate studies their identities potentially become disrupted. They enter spaces that entail re-thinking what they do and (re-)imagining what they can do in the future. Kanno and Stuart (2011), with reference to language teachers, claim that learning about teaching 'is not so much the acquisition of the knowledge of language teaching as it is the development of a teacher identity' (p. 249). The same applies to teacher educators; in the process of further and continuing professional development teacher educators' identities develop and change. In this section I examine how this happens with the group of experienced Colombian teacher educators introduced in Section 2. In that section, the teacher educators, a cohort of doctoral students at a public university, reflected on their teacher educator identities in relation to their past and present professional experiences. From their reflections I developed a list of key identity themes (see Table 1), which I then arranged into five main identity-related categories: *pedagogy, research, currency and development, context,* and *political and moral stance.* In this section, I explore their identities further by focussing particularly on their reasons for deciding to engage in further professional development in the form of formal teacher education.

The narrative interviews conducted with the teachers after their first year of study revealed that 'moving across major life boundaries' (Donato, 2017, p. 25), such as from being a teacher/teacher educator to a doctoral student/researcher, led to the transformation of their professional teacher educator identities. As the teacher educators' stories show, however, this transformation began at the time when they first started thinking about further study and was shaped by their personal reasons for wanting to make that boundary crossing. In the interviews I didn't specifically ask the teacher educators why they desired to continue their professional development in the form of a higher qualification, but they all offered their personal and professional reasons for wanting to do so. An important concept for making sense of their decisions is Norton's (2013) social construct of *investment.*

Investment refers to language learners' desire and commitment to learning a language. By investing in learning a language, they expect that they will yield some capital (some social value) as a result of that investment. An investment in learning is therefore also an investment in their identities. The construct can be applied to teacher education and teacher identity as well (see Barkhuizen, 2016). Darvin and Norton (2015) consider investment as occurring at the nexus of identity, ideology, and capital, and they claim that 'investment indexes issues of identity and imagined futures' (p. 39). Investing, in other words, means imagining the future and imaging one's identity in relation to that future world. Its relevance to the Colombian teacher educators is evident: they are investing in further teacher education in order to enhance their own capital for the various personal reasons to be discussed in the sections below. At least, this is what they anticipate when they make the decision to pursue (invest in) further professional development. Kramsch (2013, p. 195) sums up these ideas succinctly, saying investment 'accentuates the role of human agency and identity in engaging with the task at hand, in accumulating economic and symbolic capital, in having stakes in the endeavour and in persevering in that endeavour' – the task at hand being pursuing a doctoral degree to enhance one's professional development, practices, and career. In Colombia, Viáfara and Largo (2018) report that there is some reluctance for language teachers to embark on further teacher education in the form of graduate study. Although there is an expectation that they do, they see it as too theory-based, without options to guide them in how to employ that theoretical knowledge to tackle the real needs they face in schools. The teacher educators below have committed to doctoral study and the reasons they give for doing so relate directly to who they are as professionals: who they want to be and want to become; what their aspirations are for the future; what their goals are for their work, their student teachers, and their profession.

## 4.1 Teacher Educators' Reasons for Continuing Professional Development

In this section I report on the reasons the teacher educators reveal in their narrative interviews for deciding to undertake further graduate-level study. For any one participant there might be multiple reasons, as is evident in some of the short extracts below. However, in my commentary I focus on those that are most salient. The aim is to show what the reasons tell us about their transforming identities as teacher educators and the identity tensions (e.g., between their perceptions of self and ascribed identities in the midst of a period of transition) in their professional lives that contribute to that transformation. More broadly, the question these reflections address is the following: why do language teacher educators decide to continue their professional development, in this case, in the form of formal teacher education? Please refer to Section 2.1 for the short biographies of the teacher educators that immediately precede their reflections.

### 4.1.1 Juan

1  nowadays it is important to have a PhD here in Colombia
2  because the demand for PhD is increasing
3  however that was not my main motivation
4  because I don't want to be like a director
5  or like an administrative part of the administrative staff of any place
6  but I want to continue working with my students
7  and I think that was one of the motivations
8  because I feel that my Master's the Master's that I took that I studied
9  was not that strong
10  and I didn't learn as many things as I wish

Juan wants to 'continue working with my students' (line 6) when he has completed his doctorate. As a teacher educator he feels (line 8) academically behind where he should be, saying 'I didn't learn as many things as I wish' (line 10). He believes his Master's qualification (line 8) did not provide him with the necessary academic knowledge to do his job the way he would like to. His reason to study further, therefore, has to do with personal academic development in order to become a more informed teacher educator. What is interesting in his story, however, is what he says in lines 1–5. Here he comments on the importance of having a PhD in the Colombian teacher education context, meaning that to be employed full-time in a university, a doctorate is necessary (see this point articulated vociferously by Ana below). Although Juan says 'that was not my main motivation' (line 3), he is obviously aware of the pressure exerted by educational institutional authorities on their (prospective) faculty, mirroring international trends (Pereira, Lopes, & Marta, 2015). This would mean the imposition of researcher and 'director' (line 4) or 'administrative staff' (line 5) identities – identities that would compete with a teacher educator identity (see Dinkelman, 2011). Post-doctorate, Juan is not willing to sacrifice his classroom work with student teachers, and thus the teacher educator identity he claims for himself.

### 4.1.2 Yvonne

1  well I love learning
2  I mean I know that it is good to have a title
3  but I don't do it because of the title
4  I do it because I like learning
5  I do it because I think that it is an opportunity for me to re-think what I'm doing
6  how I'm doing
7  the possibility I'm having in my hand
8  what I can do for my student teachers

Yvonne's clearly stated reason in line 1, 'I love learning', contrasts sharply with a reason others might give for doing a PhD – 'to have a title' (line 2). Yvonne says, again unambiguously, 'I don't do it because of the title' (line 3). This contrast raises the tension, already expressed by Juan, between the institutional expectations for teacher educator faculty (i.e., having a PhD) and the more personal reasons they may have for entering further in-service study to prepare for those positions – expectations that may discourage or even exclude them from further study. Besides enjoying learning, Yvonne desires the 'opportunity to re-think what I'm doing' (line 5) in order to work more productively 'for my student teachers' (line 8), reflecting Juan's story. In Juan's case, however, he felt the need for a 'gap' to be filled since his Master's had not been sufficient preparation for his current work. Yvonne desires instead to invest in further study to reflect on and transform her current practice for the benefit of her student teachers.

### 4.1.3 Eduardo

1 because I wanted to

2 but that 'wanted to' means it was something for myself

3 [describes teaching experience since obtaining Master's]

4 in these six years five years

5 I felt like uncompleted

6 because I was not studying something extra

7 or apart from my studies for the subjects that I was teaching

8 and I was not learning something

9 and I said and I wanted to be academically speaking at the top of studies

10 so I wanted to study a PhD

We see here a sense of something missing in the professional, and interconnected personal, life of Eduardo. He says the doctorate is 'something for myself' (line 2) – it is for the sake of personal fulfilment. But it is also for academic advancement; he wants to be 'academically speaking at the top of studies' (line 9). Since completing his Master's he feels that he has not been learning anything new ('I was not learning something', line 8), only what he needs to know for the subjects he has been teaching. His self-perceived identity as an unfulfilled teacher educator has prompted him to pursue a doctorate. Later in his story, Eduardo reveals that his reasons also have to do with sharing his investment with his professional community, 'my knowledge of the things that I can share with others, is for others'.

### 4.1.4 Alex

1 well I started to look for a PhD after three years working at the Master's programme

2 after three years six semesters six different groups of teachers

3 I realized something there

4 and is that in my curriculum in my module of curriculum design

5 the teachers didn't have either epistemological instances

6 or pedagogical instances

7 towards teaching or learning yeah

8 because the focus of the module that I give isn't that yeah

9 what is curriculum

10 but what is curriculum from an epistemological position

11 and pedagogical position

12 well I realized that

13 and I started to look for PhDs

Alex's motivation for investing in further formal in-service study primarily has to do with advancing his knowledge of his subject area ('curriculum design', line 4). 'After three years' (line 1) teaching pre-service English teachers in a Master's programme, Alex came to the realization ('I realized something there', line 3) that the content of his curriculum design course fell short of what he expected for his student teachers at their academic level. Like the other participants, he perceived a 'gap' in an aspect of his teacher education practice. To address this situation, he 'started to look for a PhD' (line 1 and line 13) that would provide him with the relevant knowledge to develop his course so that his students would begin to explore the construct of curriculum more deeply, beyond its mere theoretical definition. His concern appears to be how we learn or acquire knowledge from curriculum ('epistemological position', line 10) and how we apply the curriculum in teaching practice ('pedagogical position', line 11). Alex has invested in further graduate teacher education therefore, not only to upskill himself, but ultimately to improve his course for the benefit of his pre-service teachers.

### 4.1.5 Diego

1  what I'm basically looking forward to is like
2  somehow allowing voices that haven't been heard
3  I don't know to what extent I could do that
4  but my intention is to fight somehow things that I consider are perpetuation of systems of injustice
5  even in terms of what languages are supposed to be
6  so language and bilingualism in Colombia has been considered from a very instrumental perspective
7  and well I have always have this idea of a language as something that is much more than that
8  is eventually part of your identity
9  and part of your rights
10  like your linguistic human rights
11  and that was something that I always felt passionate about
12  if my intention is to generate at least a change of perspective
13  like having people think again about like unfair approaches towards languages
14  and towards individuals who speak [indigenous] languages

When articulating his reason for doing further in-service graduate study, Diego's identity reveals an emotionally reinforced social justice orientation. In his powerful story he sums up the overarching goal he desires to accomplish in line 2: 'allowing voices that haven't been heard'. Through his PhD research and armed with a higher qualification he plans to 'fight' (line 4) the 'systems of injustice' (line 4) that he believes have persisted in the Colombian language education system. The main thrust of his resistance comes from his interpretation of the bilingual language policies in the country that have 'been considered from a very instrumental perspective' (line 6). By this he means that the policies support the teaching and learning of English (a colonial language) as the language of progress in employment and education, at the expense of indigenous languages (line 14), and that those who do not succeed usually find themselves on the margins of society (Wilches, Medina, & Gutiérrez, 2018). Instead, Diego believes that language is 'something that is much more than that' (line 7). It is 'part of your identity' (line 8) and 'part of your rights' (line 9). Diego feels 'passionate' (line 11) about promoting this social justice perspective in his future work and is determined through his investment in his doctoral research especially to get people to 'think again' (line 13) about these policies and their accompanying 'unfair' (line 13) practices. These people include his pre-service student teachers as well as *their* future English learners. His desire is to instil in them 'a change of perspective' (line 12) so that they can ultimately transform the 'unfair approaches towards languages' (line 13).

### *4.1.6 Ana*

1  well they opened they opened some posts
2  and I would apply for it
3  but then they said that I was not prepared
4  I mean I was not prepared because I didn't have research
5  because I didn't have this and that
6  'because your only piece of research is the one that you did for your Master's degree'
7  and I was like 'oh so I'm not enough
8  what I have done is not enough'
9  and so I said 'oh'
10  so I was thinking 'maybe I should study a PhD'
11  cause like having a Master's will never be enough
12  if I want to work in a full-time position in a university

Ana's story starts with a job application for an English teacher educator position at a university. However, her application was unsuccessful 'because I didn't have research' (line 4). As in many universities around the world, obtaining a full-time academic position as teacher educator requires research experience and a recognized publication record. Ana has neither (she says later in the story, 'I am not publishing or researching'), at least not to the extent required by the hiring institution. She does, however, have considerable experience as a language teacher. Ana's identity dilemma (Nelson, 2017) is reflected in her sarcastic outburst, 'Oh so I'm not enough/ what I have done is not enough' (lines 7–8). She knows she has considerable experience as an English teacher and adequate experience as a teacher educator, but despite having done a 'piece of research' (line 6) for her Master's degree, her researcher identity was contested by the hiring university. She did not meet their requirements for the professional position they wanted filled. To resolve this English teacher–teacher educator–researcher identity dilemma Ana decides that the best course of action would be to invest in a PhD ('maybe I should study a PhD', line 10). She realizes that without the research experience and its associated symbolic capital 'no university will accept me'.

### 4.1.7 Jenny

1  it was an accident
2  I didn't plan to do that
3  I was part of I am part of a research group
4  and the director or the coordinator
5  he told me that he was going to be in charge of one of the emphasis of the doctorate programme
6  and he invited me to be part of that
7  [summarizes previous formal study]
8  I realized that is a good opportunity to be part of a community
9  that we are creating in the doctorate programme
10  and this community is something that we don't have in Colombia

Jenny had not been searching for a PhD like Alex, and unlike the other teachers had not identified a personal or professional 'gap' in her working life that needed to be 'filled' by further in-service teacher education. Rather, she stumbled upon the possibility ('it was an accident', line 1) after having the new PhD drawn to her attention by the director of the 'doctorate program' (line 5). Jenny seized on the opportunity to be more formally part of an academic research community, pointing out that 'we don't have in Colombia' (line 10) such communities of practice. In recent years she has become a participant in various informal research groups, even establishing some herself, 'to do research, but not institutional research'. Her investment in further graduate study, therefore, at least in the short term, was also an investment in her identity as a community member of PhD research students.

## 4.2 Interconnected Identity-Related Professional Developments

All participants in this study perceive some sort of 'gap' between who they are and who they want to be (or who they think they should be) as professional teacher educators of future English teachers. It is this gap they desire to fill by embarking on further in-service graduate study. By investing in this further advanced professional development a number of things happen. They enter a period of transition in their professional lives where their familiar teacher educator identities are disrupted, (re)negotiated, and (re)constructed. As evident in the interview extracts, the teachers are aware of this change – it is what has made them decide to study further. As Donato (2017) says, they are 'creatively engaging with, responding to, and renegotiating the self in ways that contribute to one's own personal growth and development as a professional' (p. 28). Their reasons for studying further, therefore, are intimately interconnected with how they see themselves and with who they want to be in the future. Figure 2 illustrates this relationship between their *reasons* and *identity*, with *investment* or the act and goals of *investing* in further professional development connecting them together.

*Development*, the yield of their investment, emerged as a major theme in the teacher educators' stories, as can be seen in the short extracts above (and also in their longer interviews). Development means they will change as professionals – their identities will change. And development means their practices will change. To reflect these meanings, I have categorized their reasons into five types of perceived development; described below and represented by the arrow-headed lines in Figure 2 that thread through the three sectors – reasons, investment, and identity. It is probably true to say that all the teacher educators desire and

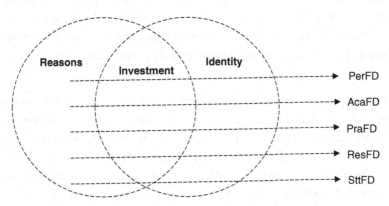

**Figure 2** Five types of identity-related professional developments.

envisage all five developments, although only one or two are explicitly referenced by each of them.

1 *Personal-focussed development (PerFD)* for doctoral students includes personal growth and the development of new skills and knowledge (see Halse & Mowbray, 2011). It comes with an increase of social and cultural capital (Norton, 2013). Yvonne says 'I love learning' and that doing the doctorate is 'an opportunity for me'. Eduardo says it is 'something for myself' and that he 'felt like uncompleted'.

2 *Academic-focussed development (AcaFD)* refers to enhanced knowledge and competences that have to do with the more theoretical aspects of teacher education. Juan says that he 'didn't learn as many things' as he wished during his Master's, and the doctorate will be an opportunity to update his knowledge, and Eduardo aims to be 'academically speaking at the top of studies'.

3 *Practice-focussed development (PraFD)* relates to practice – pedagogical practice as a teacher educator. Alex wants to learn more about curriculum theory so that he can revise 'my module of curriculum design', and Yvonne want to 're-think what I'm doing'.

4 *Research-focussed development (ResFD)* relates to both research competence – how to do research – and also how to use that competence to fulfil professional goals, such as getting published, belonging to productive research groups, and securing a full-time job. Driven by political activism, Diego's planned research has a definite social justice objective, 'allowing voices that haven't been heard'. And Ana says straightforwardly, 'I want to work in a full-time position in a university'.

5 *Student teacher-focussed development (SttFD)* is the outcome of the work that teacher educators plan to do with their pre-service teachers. Juan wants to 'continue working with my students', Yvonne says she will ascertain what she 'can do for my student teachers', Alex will improve his curriculum design course for the sake of his students, and Diego desires to encourage his future English teachers to 'generate at least a change of perspective' with regard to unfair conceptualizations of language in the Colombian educational context.

Bearing in mind these five developments, the teacher educators had high expectations of their investment to pursue further professional development. They all perceived needs in their current working lives and articulated goals for their future lives. These needs and goals are embodied in the reasons they gave for deciding to embark on doctoral studies, and are thus tied to their professional identities. Furthermore, identities are nearly always constructed in and through emotional experience (Miller & Gkonou, 2018). For example,

Ana expressed frustration and possibly anger at the hiring university's requirement for research and for not valuing her extensive teaching experience.
Diego feels 'passionate' about linguistic human rights. Yvonne says 'I love
learning', and Jenny is excited about being part of a research community. In
answer to the question, then, posed at the beginning of this section, *why do
language teacher educators decide to continue their professional development, in this case, in the form of formal teacher education?*, it is to invest in
further education to meet needs and achieve goals and to develop personally
and professionally in all or some of the five ways described above. It also
means investing in identity (Norton, 2013) and navigating the associated
emotions through which the identities are constructed. Although the focus in
this section has been on the experiences of a cohort of English language
teacher educators practising in Colombia, much of what was found in terms
of their reasons, identities, and desired developments is probably applicable to
language teacher educators in other contexts too.

## 5 Future Research on Language Teacher Educator Identity

This section offers forty questions to encourage further research into the lives
and identities of language teacher educators. The questions are not meant to be
unalterable research questions to be taken up wholeheartedly within a particular
study. Instead, I hope that they prompt reflection (and suitable adaptation) on the
part of researchers who might be interested in exploring further the field of
language teacher education, particularly the identity of language teacher educators. Language teacher educators might also wish to consult the questions for
the purposes of self-inquiring into their own professional experiences and
development. Coming up with a research topic (see Barkhuizen, 2019b) is not
simply a matter of finding a question and investigating it in one's particular
context. Researchers need to draw on their own experience, consider their own
knowledge and skills, ascertain the appropriateness of the question to their
context, and evaluate practical conditions such as equipment and other
resources. Nevertheless, as I say, I hope that the following questions suggest
possible research topics that might be of interest and use to the scholarly work of
those working in this field. I have divided Section 5 into four parts. The first
focusses on beginning language teacher educators and suggests some key
concepts relevant to early career teacher educators that could be explored
further. The second addresses conceptualizations of language teacher educator
identity, and the next suggests questions relating to the work of teacher educators in the areas of pedagogy, research, and service. The final section concludes
this Element.

## 5.1 Beginning Language Teacher Educators

In this section I draw on an induction framework (Barkhuizen, 2002) that helps to explain the early experiences of entering a new professional role. I use key concepts from that framework to suggest the first ten questions. Becoming a teacher educator or taking on a teacher educator role for the first time, such as mentoring student teachers on a practicum experience or conducting a series of professional development workshops for teachers, always leads to a certain amount of tension or *instability* in the teacher educators' lives. Bateson (1972) refers to instability in life in general, saying that people are self-corrective systems. By this he means that people adjust to instability or transitions in order to achieve equilibrium. In other words, when people experience 'disequilibrium' or instability in their lives, they strive to self-correct in order to once again achieve stability.

I have used the term *coping* in educational contexts to describe this self-correction, which could be cognitive (e.g., rationalizing or attempting to understand the situation) or an activity (e.g., doing something about the cause of the instability). Coping can be of two kinds. The first is *instability-reducing*, which describes thinking or actions that reduce or constrain perceived instability in educational contexts.

**Q1**: *What do institution-based language teacher educators do to reduce instability in their institutional lives during their first year as a teacher educator? How does what they do relate to their developing teacher educator identity?*
**Q2**: *How do teacher educators cope in achieving their pedagogical aims in linguistically diverse classes of pre-service English teachers? How does their developing teacher educator identity relate to their coping?*

Instability could also be prevented before it occurs. This thinking or activity is therefore referred to as *instability-preventing*, and occurs in situations where one anticipates a state of tension or instability and acts to prevent it before it occurs.

**Q3**: *What strategies do language teacher educators employ in their pedagogy when their language is different from the institutional medium of instruction, and different from the language of the majority of their student teachers? What do their instability-preventing strategies say about their perceptions of their and their teachers' identities?*
**Q4**: *What effect does an unexpected, sudden curriculum change (e.g., moving teacher training online; implementing a new assessment regime) have on the planning and practices of a teacher educator? How does it affect their emotions and sense of self-efficacy?*

Fairclough (1989), referring to his concept of discourse, says that 'each discourse type establishes its particular set of subject positions, which those who operate within it are constrained to occupy' (p. 102). I refer to this process as *conforming*. Conforming implies change; there is a movement towards fitting in, towards doing something differently or, perhaps, towards becoming like someone else. This means that although teacher educators may not intend to act in a certain way, or may not have expected to act in some way, they do, and these actions become recurring in their lives as teacher educators.

**Q5**: *How does a language teacher educator new to a particular context display conforming practices during their first semester or year as a teacher educator, or over the course of a professional development programme? What effect does this have on their professional identity?*
**Q6**: *How does the conforming of language teacher educators vary over the course of their careers? Do their identities align with their changing levels of conforming?*

*Generating* is the development of new beliefs or practices that are part of the working life of teacher educators. To generate is to try something new, to try some alternative or something opposite to one's established, usual patterns of practice. Teacher educators innovate all the time, sometimes consciously and sometimes unconsciously, especially during the early part of their careers as they learn about teacher education and construct new identities. To prevent or reduce instability is not to generate; that would be coping.

**Q7**: *How does teaching a particular language teaching innovation to student teachers unfold over time in a teacher education course or programme? What is the role and responsibility of the teacher educator, and what identities are exposed and hidden during the innovation process?*
**Q8**: *What risks are involved in not being seen to be a generating language teacher educator (e.g., personal, professional, institutional)? What are the advantages of being recognized as a generating language teacher educator?*

I use the term *opposing* to refer to thinking and acting that goes against the existing system (or agenda or ground rules) of the institutional workplace or its professional teacher education practices, negating them and valuing their opposite. This thinking and acting, however, stays within the existing framework: the teacher educator operates or opposes within the existing system. If, for example, the practice of a teacher education department is to require its faculty to use only English in its classes, and a teacher educator believes that would be unfair on some student teachers and a waste of class time and therefore decides not to follow this rule, this would be opposing activity.

**Q9**: *How might practising opposing behaviour make a language teacher educator feel as a professional? How do these opposing acts become visible to teacher educators' colleagues in a programme and how do they make them feel?*

**Q10**: *Do poor student teacher evaluations lead to opposing practices from language teacher educators? What are some sources of opposing thinking and activity in a teacher education programme?*

*Resisting* means thinking and acting differently, rejecting the existing system (or agenda or ground rules) of the institutional workplace or its professional teacher education practices, and at the same time actively attempting to change the system. So, resisting is going a step further than opposing. To continue with the English-only example, if the opposing teacher educator manages to convince the whole department of the futility of the practice, and the department decides to discontinue the requirement of using only English in its classes, then the teacher educator would have exhibited resisting practices.

**Q11**: *Does foregrounding language teacher educator's social identities 'open up new spaces for agency and critique of existing structures, and create new possibilities for the ways in which our students understand themselves and enact their teaching' (Peercy et al., 2019, p. 12)?*

**Q12**: *Reform, re-structuring, and re-organizing are words often heard in the corridors of neoliberal institutions of higher education. How might language teacher educators become involved in such activities or how and why might they actively resist participation?*

## 5.2 Defining Language Teacher Educators

In my edited book, *Reflections on Language Teacher Identity Research* (Barkhuizen, 2017), I thematically analyzed all the chapters in which the forty-one authors reflected on their perceptions of language teacher identity in their area of scholarly expertise, to produce a composite conceptualization of teacher identity – a broad 'definition' that aimed to capture the various theoretical perspectives on language *teacher* identity drawn from the ideas in the chapters. The conceptualization captures many of the ideas relating to language *teacher educator* identity presented so far in this Element, so I present it here, slightly adapted (p. 4):

> Language teacher educator identities are cognitive, social, emotional, ideological, and historical – they are both inside the teacher and outside in the

social, material and technological world. Language teacher educator identities are being and doing, feeling and imagining, and storying. They are struggle and harmony: they are contested and resisted, by self and others, and they are also accepted, acknowledged and valued, by self and others. They are core and peripheral, personal and professional, they are dynamic, multiple, and hybrid, and they are foregrounded and backgrounded. And language teacher educator identities change, short-term and over time – discursively in social interaction with pre- and in-service teachers, other teacher educators, language learners, administrators, and the wider community, and in material interaction with spaces, places and objects in classrooms, institutions, and online.

I suggest in the book that this composite conceptualization be interpreted variously from different theoretical perspectives as well as from different contextual realities (e.g., spaces where teacher education and language teaching are practised). Here I suggest in addition that the conceptualization serves as a stimulus to generate research questions in these contexts, and list the following as possible avenues for further investigation.

**Q13**: *How are language teacher educators perceived by colleagues in other disciplines and by management in their institutions? What professional identities are ascribed to them, and how does this make them feel?*

**Q14**: *How do language teacher educators' intersecting identities inform who they are in the classroom and how does this shape what they do and how they are perceived by their student teachers?*

**Q15**: *In what ways do language teacher educators 'story' their professional experiences? What do the stories they tell about their teaching, research, and service say about their identities at particular times and in particular places?*

**Q16**: *What would a typology of language teacher educators look like? Who would be included and who would be excluded? What would the selection criteria be?*

**Q17**: *What are the main similarities and differences between a language teacher identity and a language teacher educator identity? How do we find out?*

**Q18**: *How should induction programmes for new language teacher educators take into account their professional identities? What should institutions do to acknowledge and work with their identities in the planning and implementation of these programmes?*

**Q19**: *How feasible is it for language teacher educators to use 'identity as an organizing framework to understand their practices and potential venues for ongoing growth' (Yazan, 2018, p. 152)? What do language teacher educators find the strengths and limitations of this approach to be?*

**Q20**: *Teacher educators' identities are 'struggle and harmony'. In a world where social justice and well-being are becoming more embedded in* *institutional policies and professional practices, how do language teacher educators ensure that they take care of themselves in the course of their teacher education work?*

## 5.3 Being Language Teacher Educators

I categorize this final set of questions according to the four domains of language teacher educators' identity work illustrated in Figure 1 (see Section 3.3).

### 5.3.1 Pedagogy

**Q21**: *How does and what type of student teacher engagement in the activities assigned and mediated by language teacher educators influence what and how they learn? What role does the teacher educators' identity play in this pedagogy?*
**Q22**: *How do language teacher educators make space for and legitimize student teachers' voices in their teacher education classes? What is their approach to opening up these spaces and how do they negotiate for their own professional identities to enter those spaces?*
**Q23**: *What approaches do language teacher educators use to ensure their student teachers develop the knowledge and skills necessary to apply their teaching education learning to their real-school language learning contexts?*
**Q24**: *How are language teacher educators 'complicit in maintaining structures and discourses that produce and reproduce inequities' (*Peercy et al., 2019, p. 12*)? What do their identities have to do with this?*
**Q25**: *What metaphors are used to describe the teaching practices and pedagogical identities of language teacher educators?*

### 5.3.2 Research

**Q26**: *How important is a researcher identity to language teacher educators working in different roles (e.g., mentor of practicum student teachers, research supervisor, university academic) in different contexts?*
**Q27**: *How do language teacher educators balance institutional requirements and responsibilities and personal desires and preferences with regard to research activity, engagement, and productivity? How do their researcher identity and pedagogy identity interrelate?*
**Q28**: *How does self-study (*Peercy & Sharkey, 2020*) contribute to a deeper understanding of the language teacher educator as practitioner and researcher over a period of time?*

**Q29**: *How do interactions between student teacher researchers and teacher educator (research supervisory meetings, mediations, consultations) lead to learning about research? What kind of learning emerges from the interactions? What identities do language teacher educators negotiate during these interactions?*

**Q30**: *To what extent do very experienced researchers with little to no interaction with classroom language teachers or pre-service teachers identify as language teacher educators?*

### 5.3.3 Institutional Service and Leadership

**Q31**: *In higher education institutional settings, in what ways are language teacher educators 'a particular type of academic' (*Murray & Male, 2005)*? What is it that they do that makes them different from other academics?*

**Q32**: *How does a language teacher educator become a manager of a programme, department, or school, and how do they practise as a manager and feel about being a manager? Does managing distance them from their teacher educator identities?*

**Q33**: *How is 'service' defined in a particular programme or institution, and how does this definition apply to language teacher educators compared with colleagues in other disciplines? Is there such a thing as a language teacher educator service identity?*

**Q34**: *How might a language teacher educator lead the design of a teacher education programme that, being committed to social justice and equity in language teaching, takes into account 'why we teach languages, what languages we teach, and how we teach languages' (*Gao, 2019, p. 165)*?*

**Q35**: *How can language teacher educators instil in their teachers the importance of making a service contribution to their courses, programmes and institutions? Should they, and what might the nature of these service contributions be?*

### 5.3.4 Community Service and Leadership

**Q36**: *'The impact of globalization has in recent years given rise to a healthy debate in TESOL regarding the peculiar nature of English as a global language, its imperialist features (both colonial and neo-imperialist) and its impact worldwide' (*Hayes, 2005, p. 190)*. How does the meaning of this statement influence the community work of a language teacher educator or team of educators working in a particular geopolitical context?*

**Q37**: *What do language teacher educators gain from participating in local language teacher conferences and how can they contribute?*

**Q38**: *What are the experiences of language teacher educators who have contributed to language-in-education policy debates at government level? How did they contribute, and what were the outcomes? How were they perceived by stakeholders from outside the educational context?*

**Q39**: *What kind of work do language teacher educators do in professional language teaching associations? What is the perceived value of their contributions and how are they perceived by other members?*

**Q40**: *How important is it to have 'good leaders' for the development of the language teaching profession? What do language teacher educators have to do to become those leaders?*

---

PERSONAL NARRATIVE 5: DEVELOPING A RESEARCHER IDENTITY

When do you feel you are a researcher? At what point in your career do you think that part of what you do as a professional is research? That you have a researcher identity? These are questions I constantly ask myself, even after many years of being a teacher educator and doing research. I had to do research to gain a doctorate. When I was a high school teacher (post-doctorate) I did no research – I was too busy teaching English. When I got my first full-time university position I had to do research – it was in my contract. When did this having to do research cross over to being something that I did because it was my choice or because I saw a need or a gap to be filled? When I did my doctoral research I thoroughly enjoyed it. I investigated the classroom experiences of a first-year ESL teacher during the first six weeks of her teaching career in a New York City high school. I was fascinated. I couldn't wait to observe her classes and to interview her. I loved analyzing the transcripts, word by word, and found the writing-up process intriguing (why do it this way and not that way?). I didn't think at the time I was fulfilling any particular need, or making any contributions to anything. I was doing the research for a qualification, learning a lot in the process, and, incidentally, being of some support to the new teacher during a particularly challenging time for her. A few years later I was living in South Africa during the time apartheid was being dismantled. Educational institutions were becoming racially integrated, and therefore multilingual, including schools and universities. This situation was therefore ripe for linguistic investigation, and there was an urgent need to understand what was happening in these institutions to inform policy and curriculum decisions. My research attention therefore turned to investigating the language practices and learning in these institutions. Of course I found the research interesting, but this time I was responding to a need (and, since I was working at a university, I was also fulfilling my institutional research obligations). The balancing of *passion* and *need* – a personal desire and interest in research, and an obligation or response to a societal or educational need – is a constant tension in my researcher identity. The ideal way to resolve the *passion* versus *need* dilemma is to focus on research questions that achieve *both*; that is, they ask about topics one is passionate about and they also fulfil some community or institutional need. This is a balance I have tried to achieve throughout my research career. It is what keeps my researcher identity vital, it allows for easy and useful transfer of my research findings to my teacher education pedagogy, and it maintains my motivation to keep on researching.

## 5.4 Conclusion

To conclude this Element I return to the beginning, where I declared that *language teacher educators teach teachers how to teach language*, and commented that although this statement sounds somewhat simple, a closer examination immediately raises questions; questions to do with the *teachers* who participate in teacher education, the *contexts* in which teacher education occurs, and the *language teacher educators* who are pivotal in the whole process. This Element has attempted to address some of these questions, and may even have answered some along the way. What it has shown is that the lives of language teacher educators are extremely varied. Any one teacher educator working across time and place will change the work they do, and in the process they too will change. And different teacher educators working in different contexts can be doing very different things but all call themselves language teacher educators. Characteristic of their work is pedagogy, research, and service (institutional and community), and working across these domains with their own communities means that teacher educators are constantly negotiating their multiple identities to position themselves where they want to be or do not want to be. At the same time they are being positioned by others – their student teachers, colleagues, and institutions. This Element has tried to show what identities language teacher educators construct in this process, how these relate to the different types of language teacher educators there are in the field, and what sort of work teacher educators do as they construct and enact their identities. A number of researchers have commented that language teacher educators have been neglected in the research literature in language teaching and learning. I hope that this Element has highlighted the need to focus attention on the work they do and signalled the broad scope of scholarly potential that exists to be investigated, particularly that in relation to the development of their identities. Perhaps the forty questions asked in Section 5 give some indication of the way forward.

# 6 References

Al-Issa, A. S. M. (2017). Qualities of the professional English language teacher educator: Implications for achieving quality and accountability. *Cogent Education*, 4, 1326652. https://doi.org/10.1080/2331186X.2017.1326652.

Amott, P., & Ang, L. (2020). (Re)thinking teacher educator professional identity. In M. A. Peters (Ed.), *Encyclopedia of Teacher Education* (pp. 1–6). https://doi.org/10.1007/978–981-13–1179-6_381–1.

Barkhuizen, G. (2002). Beginning to lecture at university: A complex web of socialisation patterns. *Higher Education Research and Development*, 21(1), 93–109.

Barkhuizen, G. (2016). A short story approach to analyzing teacher (imagined) identities over time. *TESOL Quarterly*, 50(3), 655–83.

Barkhuizen, G. (Ed.) (2017). *Reflections on Language Teacher Identity Research*. New York: Routledge.

Barkhuizen, G. (2019a). Teacher identity. In S. Walsh & S. Mann (Eds.), *The Routledge Handbook of English Language Teacher Education* (pp. 536–52). Abingdon: Routledge.

Barkhuizen, G. (Ed.) (2019b). *Qualitative Research Topics in Language Teacher Education*. New York: Routledge.

Barkhuizen, G. (2020a). Identity dilemmas of a teacher (educator) researcher: Teacher research versus academic institutional research. *Educational Action Research*. https://doi.org/10.1080/09650792.2020.1842779.

Barkhuizen, G. (2020b). Core dimensions of narrative inquiry. In J. McKinley & H. Rose (Eds.), *The Routledge Handbook of Research Methods in Applied Linguistics* (pp. 188–98). Abingdon: Routledge.

Bateson, G. (1972). *Steps to an Ecology of Mind*. New York: Ballentine.

Bégin, C., & Gérard, L. (2013). The role of supervisors in light of the experience of doctoral students. *Policy Futures in Education*, 11(3), 267–76.

Békés, E. A. (2020). Supporting Ecuadorian teachers in their classroom research: Reflections on becoming a research mentor. *English Language Teaching and Research Journal*, 2(1), 27–45.

Billot, J. (2010). The imagined and the real: Identifying the tensions for academic identity. *Higher Education Research and Development*, 29(6), 709–21.

Block, D. (2013). Issues in language and identity research in applied linguistics. *Estudios Lingüística Inglesa Aplicada*, 13, 11–46.

Bolitho, R. (2020, February). Stages in an English teacher's career and some of the dilemmas and questions that accompany each stage. *Humanising Language*

*Teaching*, 4–8. www.hltmag.co.uk/feb2020/rethinking-language-teacher-training (last accessed 9 April 2020).

Boylan, M., & Woolsey, I. (2015). Teacher education for social justice: Mapping identity spaces. *Teaching and Teacher Education*, 46, 62–71.

Brancard, R., & QuinnWilliams, J. (2012). Learning labs: Collaborations for transformative teacher learning. *TESOL Journal*, 3(3), 320–49.

British Council (2017). *Continuing Professional Development (CPD) Framework for Teacher Educators*. www.teachingenglish.org.uk/sites/tea cheng/files/Teacher%20Educator%20Framework%20FINAL%20WEBv1 .pdf (last accessed 10 March 2020).

Bullough, R. V. (2005). Being and becoming a mentor: School-based teacher educators and teacher educator identity. *Teaching and Teacher Education*, 21 (2), 143–55.

Canagarajah, S. (2017). Multilingual identity in teaching multilingual writing. In G. Barkhuizen (Ed.), *Reflections on Language Teacher Identity Research* (pp. 67–73). New York: Routledge.

Casanave, C. P., & Schecter, S. R. (Eds.) (1997). *On Becoming a Language Educator: Personal Essays on Professional Development*. Mahwah, NJ: Lawrence Erlbaum.

Chase, S. E. (2003). Learning to listen: Narrative principles in a qualitative research methods course. In R. Josselson, A. Lieblich, & D. P. McAdams (Eds.), *Up Close and Personal: The Teaching and Learning of Narrative Research* (pp. 79–99). Washington DC: American Psychological Association.

Clarke, M. A. (2019). Creating contexts for teacher development. In S. Walsh & S. Mann (Eds.), *The Routledge Handbook of English Language Teacher Education* (pp. 365–82). Abingdon: Routledge.

Cochran-Smith, M. (2005). Teacher educators as researchers: Multiple perspectives. *Teaching and Teacher Education*, 21, 219–25.

Darvin, R., & Norton, B. (2015). Identity and a model of investment in applied linguistics. *Annual Review of Applied Linguistics*, 35, 36–56.

Davey, R. (2013). *The Professional Identity of Teacher Educators: Career on the Cusp?* Abingdon: Routledge.

Day, C. (1999). *Developing Teachers: The Challenges of Lifelong Learning*. London: Falmer Press.

De Costa, P. I., & Norton, B. (2017). Introduction: Identity, transdisciplinarity, and the good language teacher. *The Modern Language Journal*, 101(S), 3–14.

De Stefani, M. (2019). Leadership and language teacher development. In S. Walsh & S. Mann (Eds.), *The Routledge Handbook of English Language Teacher Education* (pp. 596–610). Abingdon: Routledge.

Dinkelman, T. (2011). Forming a teacher educator identity: Uncertain standards, practices and relationships. *Journal of Education and Teaching*, 37, 309–23.

Domínguez, M. (2019). Decolonial innovation in teacher development: Praxis beyond the colonial zero-point. *Journal of Education and Teaching*, 45(1), 47–62.

Donato, R. (2017). Becoming a language teaching professional: What's identity got to do with it? In G. Barkhuizen (Ed.), *Reflections on Language Teacher Identity Research* (pp. 24–30). New York: Routledge.

Douglas Fir Group (2016). A transdisciplinary framework for SLA in a multilingual world. *The Modern Language Journal*, 100(S), 19–47.

Fairclough, N. (1989). *Language and Power*. London: Longman.

Fanselow, J. F., & Hiratsuka, T. (2019). Suggestions for teacher educators from a gentle iconoclast and a fellow explorer. In S. Walsh & S. Mann (Eds.), *The Routledge Handbook of English Language Teacher Education* (pp. 96–108). Abingdon: Routledge.

Farrell, T. S. C. (2008). Here's the book, go teach the class: ELT practicum support. *RELC Journal*, 39, 226–41.

Farrell, T. S. C. (Ed.) (2015). *International Perspectives on English Language Teacher Education: Innovations From the Field*. Basingstoke: Palgrave Macmillan.

Farrell, T. S. C. (2018). Second language teacher education and future directions. In J. I. Liontas (Ed.), *The TESOL Encyclopedia of English Language Teaching*. Hoboken, NJ: John Wiley & Sons. https://doi.org/10.1002/9781118784235.eelt0922.

Farrell, T. S. C., Baurain, B., & Lewis, M. (2020). 'We teach who we are': Contemplation, reflective practice and spirituality in TESOL. *RELC Journal*, May. https://doi.org/10.1177/0033688220915647.

Freeman, D. (1989). Teacher training, development, and decision making: A model of teaching and related strategies for language teacher education. *TESOL Quarterly*, 23(1), 27–45.

Freeman, D. (2016). *Educating Second Language Teachers*. Oxford: Oxford University Press.

Freeman, D., Webre, A.-C., & Epperson, M. (2019). What counts as knowledge in English language teaching? In S. Walsh & S. Mann (Eds.), *The Routledge Handbook of English Language Teacher Education* (pp. 13–24). Abingdon: Routledge.

Gao, X. (2019). The Douglas Fir Group Framework as a resource map for language teacher education. *The Modern Language Journal*, 103(S1), 161–6.

Gee, J. P. (2000). Identity as an analytic lens for research in education. *Review of Research in Education*, 25, 99–125.

Gkonou, C., & Miller, E. R. (2020). 'Critical incidents' in language teachers' narratives of emotional experience. In C. Gkonou, J.-M. Dewaele & J. King (Eds.), *The Emotional Rollercoaster of Language Teaching* (pp. 131–49). Bristol: Multilingual Matters.

Golombek, P. R. (2017). Innovating my thinking and practices as a language teacher educator through my work as a researcher. In T. S. Gregersen & P. D. MacIntyre (Eds.), *Innovative Practices in Language Teacher Education* (pp. 15–31). Rotterdam, The Netherlands: Springer.

Gómez-Vásquez, L. Y., & Guerrero Nieto, C. H. (2018). Non-native English speaking teachers' subjectivities and Colombian language policies: A narrative study. *Profile*, 29(2), 51–64.

Goodwin, A. L., Smith, L., Souto-Manning, M., Cheruvu, R., Tan, M. Y., Reed, R., & Taveras, L. (2014). What should teacher educators know and be able to do? Perspectives from practicing teacher educators. *Journal of Teacher Education*, 65(4), 284–302.

Grassick, L. (2019). Supporting the development of primary in-service teacher educators. *ELT Journal*, 73(4), 428–37.

Gray, J., & Morton, T. (2018). *Social Interaction and English Language Teacher Identity*. Edinburgh: Edinburgh University Press.

Hacker, P. (2008). Understanding the nature of language teacher educator learning: Substance, narrative essence, and contextual reality. Unpublished doctoral thesis, University of Auckland, New Zealand.

Halse, C. (2011). Becoming a supervisor: The impact of doctoral supervision on supervisors' learning. *Studies in Higher Education*, 36(5), 557–70.

Halse, C., & Mowbray, S. (2011). The impact of the doctorate. *Studies in Higher Education*, 36, 513–25.

Hayes, D. (2005). Exploring the lives of non-native speaking English educators in Sri Lanka. *Teachers and Teaching: Theory and Practice*, 11(2), 169–94.

Hayes, D. (2019). Continuing professional development/continuous professional learning for English language teachers. In S. Walsh & S. Mann (Eds.), *The Routledge Handbook of English Language Teacher Education* (pp. 155–68). Abingdon: Routledge.

Hökkä, P., Vähäsantanen, K., & Mahlakaarto, S. (2017). Teacher educators' collective professional agency and identity: Transforming marginality to strength. *Teaching and Teacher Education*, 63, 36–46.

Johnson, K. E., & Golombek, P. (2020). Informing and transforming language teacher education pedagogy. *Language Teaching Research*, 24(1), 116–27.

Kani, Z. G. (2014). English language teacher educators' 'real world' approaches to professional learning. *Procedia: Social and Behavioral Sciences*, 116, 4080–5.

Kanno, Y., & Stuart, C. (2011). Learning to become a second language teacher: Identities-in-practice. *The Modern Language Journal*, 95(2), 236–52.

Kramp, M. K. (2004). Exploring life and experience through narrative inquiry. In K. deMarrais & S. D. Lapan (Eds.), *Foundations for Research: Methods of Inquiry in Education and the Social Sciences* (pp. 103–21). Mahwah, NJ: Erlbaum.

Kramsch, C. J. (2013). Afterword. In B. Norton, *Identity and Language Learning: Extending the Conversation* (2nd edition) (pp. 192–201). Bristol: Multilingual Matters.

Kubanyiova, M. (2020). Language teacher education in the age of ambiguity: Educating responsive meaning makers in the world. *Language Teaching Research*, 24(1), 49–59.

Lindahl, K., & Yazan, B. (Eds.) (2019). Special issue of *TESOL Journal*. An identity-oriented lens to TESOL teachers' lives: From teacher education to classroom contexts. *TESOL Journal*, 10(4). https://doi.org/10.1002/tesj.506.

Lortie, D. C. (1975). *Schoolteacher: A Sociological Study*. Chicago, IL: University of Chicago Press.

Loughran, J. (2014). Professionally developing as a teacher educator. *Journal of Teacher Education*, 65(4), 271–83.

Lunenberg, M., Dengerink, J., & Korthagen F. (2014). *The Professional Teacher Educator: Roles, Behaviour, and Professional Development of Teacher Educators*. Rotterdam, The Netherlands: Sense Publishers.

Lunenberg, M., Korthagen, F., & Swennen, A. (2007). The teacher educator as a role model. *Teaching and Teacher Education*, 23, 586–601.

Maley, A. (Ed.) (2019). *Developing Expertise Through Experience*. London: British Council.

Malm, B. (2020). On the complexities of educating student teachers: Teacher educators' views on contemporary challenges to their profession. *Journal of Education for Teaching*, 46(3), 351–64.

McKeon, F., & Harrison, J. (2010). Developing pedagogical practice and professional identities of beginning teacher educators. *Professional Development in Education*, 36(1–2), 25–44.

Mendieta, J., & Barkhuizen, G. (2020). Blended language learning in the Colombian context: A narrative inquiry of teacher ownership of curriculum change. *Computer Assisted Language Learning* 33(3), 176–96.

Miller, E. R., & Gkonou, C. (2018). Language teacher agency, emotion labor and emotional rewards in tertiary-level English language classes. *System: An International Journal of Educational Technology and Applied Linguistics*, 79, 49–59.

Miller, E. R., Morgan, B., & Medina, A. L. (2017). Exploring English teacher identity work as ethical self-formation. *The Modern Language Journal*, 101 (S1), 91–105.

Moradkhani, S., Akbari, R., Samar, R. G., & Kiany, G. R. (2013). English language teacher educators' pedagogical knowledge base: The macro and micro categories. *Australian Journal of Teacher Education*, 38(10), 123–41.

Morgan, B. (2004). Teacher identity as pedagogy: Towards a field-internal conceptualisation in bilingual and second language education. *International Journal of Bilingual Education and Bilingualism*, 7, 172–88.

Motha, S. (2014). *Race, Empire, and English Language Teaching: Creating Responsible and Ethical Anti-Racist Practices*. New York: Teachers College Press.

Motteram, G., & Dawson, S. (2019). *Resilience and Language Teacher Development in Challenging Contexts: Supporting Teachers Through Social Media*. London: British Council.

Murray, J., & Male, T. (2005). Becoming a teacher educator: Evidence from the field. *Teaching and Teacher Education*, 21, 125–42.

Nagatomo, D. H. (2012). *Exploring Japanese University English Teachers' Professional Identity*. Bristol: Multilingual Matters.

Nelson, C. D. (2017). Identity dilemmas and research agendas. In G. Barkhuizen (Ed.), *Reflections on Language Teacher Identity Research* (pp. 234–9). New York: Routledge.

Nguyen, H. T. M. (2017). *Models of Mentoring in Language Teacher Education*. Cham, Switzerland: Springer.

Norton, B. (2013). *Identity and Language Learning: Extending the Conversation* (2nd edition). Bristol: Multilingual Matters.

Padwad, A., & Parnham, J. (2019). Teacher networks in the wild: Alternative ways of professional development. In S. Walsh & S. Mann (Eds.), *The Routledge Handbook of English Language Teacher Education* (pp. 553–69). Abingdon: Routledge.

Peercy, M. M., & Sharkey, J. (2020). Missing a S-STEP? How self-study of teacher education practice can support the language teacher education knowledge base. *Language Teaching Research*, 24(1), 105–15.

Peercy, M. M., Sharkey, J., Baecher, L., Motha, S., & Varghese, M. (2019). Exploring TESOL teacher educators as learners and reflective scholars: A shared narrative inquiry. *TESOL Journal*, 10(4), e482. https://doi.org/10 .1002/tesj.482.

Pereira, F., Lopes, A., & Marta, M. (2015). Being a teacher educator: Professional identities and conceptions of professional education. *Educational Research*, 57(4), 451–69.

Richards, J., & Farrell, T. (2005). *Professional Development for Language Teachers: Strategies for Teacher Learning*. Cambridge: Cambridge University Press.

Shah, S. R. (2017). The significance of teacher leadership in TESOL: A theoretical perspective. *Arab World English Journal*, 8(4), 240–58.

Smith, J., Rattray, J., Peseta, T., & Loads, D. (2016). *Identity Work in the Contemporary University: Exploring an Uneasy Profession*. Rotterdam, The Netherlands: Sense Publishers.

Smith, K. (2005). Teacher educators' expertise: What do novice teachers and teacher educators say? *Teaching and Teacher Education*, 21, 177–92.

Smith, R. (2020). *Mentoring Teachers to Research Their Classrooms: A Practical Handbook*. New Delhi, India: The British Council.

Teemant, A. (2020). Reframing the space between: Teachers and learners in context. *Language Teaching Research*, 24(1), 82–93.

Trent, J. (2013). Becoming a teacher educator: The multiple boundary-crossing experiences of beginning teacher educators. *Journal of Teacher Education*, 64(3), 262–75.

Vaillant, D. (2011). Preparing teachers for inclusive education in Latin America. *Prospects*, 41(3), 385–98.

Vanassche, E., & Kelchtermans, G. (2016). A narrative analysis of a teacher educator's professional learning journey. *European Journal of Teacher Education*, 39(3), 355–67.

Van Lankveld, T., Schoonenboom, J., Volman, M., Croiset, G., & Beishuizen, J. (2017). Developing a teacher identity in the university context: A systematic review of the literature. *Higher Education Research and Development*, 36(2), 325–42.

Varghese, M. (2017). Language teacher educator identity and language teacher identity: Towards a social justice perspective. In G. Barkhuizen (Ed.), *Reflections on Language Teacher Identity Research* (pp. 43–8). New York: Routledge.

Varghese, M., Motha, S., Trent, J., Park, G., & Reeves, J. (Eds.) (2016). Language teacher identity in multilingual settings (Special issue). *TESOL Quarterly*, 50(3), 541–783.

Viáfara, J. J., & Largo, J. D. (2018). Colombian English teachers' professional development: The case of master programs. *Profile*, 20(1), 103–19.

Wang, H., & Mantero, M. (2018). International teaching assistants' professional identity development in the United States: A multiple case study perspective. *EFL Journal*, 3(1), 23–43.

Wilches, J. A. U., Medina, J. M. O., & Gutiérrez, C. (2018). Indigenous students learning English in higher education: Challenges and hopes. *Íkala, Journal of Language and Culture*, 23, 229–54.

Williams, J. (2014). Teacher educator professional learning in the third space: Implications for identity and practice. *Journal of Teacher Education*, 65(4), 315–26.

Williams, J., Ritter, J., & Bullock, S. M. (2012). Understanding the complexity of becoming a teacher educator: Experience, belonging, and practice within a professional learning community. *Studying Teacher Education*, 8(3), 245–60.

Wood, D., & Borg, T. (2010). The rocky road: The journey from classroom teacher to teacher educator. *Studying Teacher Education*, 6(1), 17–28.

Wright, T. (2010). Second language teacher education: Review of recent research on practice. *Language Teaching*, 43(3), 259–96.

Wright, T., & Bolitho, R. (2007). *Trainer Development*. www.lulu.com (last accessed 18 July 2020).

Yan, C., & He, C. (2010). Transforming the existing model of teaching practicum: A study of Chinese EFL student teachers' perceptions. *Journal of Education for Teaching*, 36(1), 57–73.

Yazan, B. (2018). TESL teacher educators' professional self-development, identity, and agency. *TESL Canada Journal*, 35(2), 140–55.

Yazan, B. (2019). Identities and ideologies in a language teacher candidate's autoethnography: Making meaning of stories experience. *TESOL Journal*, 10 (4), e500. https://doi.org/10.1002/tesj.500.

Yazan, B., & Lindahl, K. (Eds.) (2020). *Language Teacher Identity in TESOL: Teacher Education and Practice as Identity Work*. New York: Routledge.

Zeichner, K. (2010). Rethinking the connections between campus courses and field experiences in college- and university-based teacher education. *Journal of Teacher Education*, 61(1–2), 89–99.

# Acknowledgements

Thank you to the language teacher educators from Colombia and to Harold Castañeda-Peña for his collaboration. Thanks also to Manka Varghese and Jagadish Paudel for sharing documents and conversations, and to the two reviewers of the manuscript for their careful reading and useful comments.

# Elements in Language Teaching

### Heath Rose, *Linacre College, University of Oxford*

Heath Rose is an Associate Professor of Applied Linguistics at the University of Oxford. At Oxford, he is course director of the MSc in Applied Linguistics for Language Teaching. Before moving into academia, Heath worked as a language teacher in Australia and Japan in both school and university contexts. He is author of numerous books, such as Introducing Global Englishes, The Japanese Writing System, Data Collection Research Methods in Applied Linguistics, and Global Englishes for Language Teaching. Heath's research interests are firmly situated within the field of second language teaching, and include work on Global Englishes, teaching English as an international language, and English Medium Instruction.

### Jim McKinley, *University College London*

Jim McKinley is an Associate Professor of Applied Linguistics and TESOL at UCL, Institute of Education, where he serves as Academic Head of Learning and Teaching. His major research areas are second language writing in global contexts, the internationalisation of higher education, and the relationship between teaching and research. Jim has edited or authored numerous books including the Routledge Handbook of Research Methods in Applied Linguistics, Data Collection Research Methods in Applied Linguistics, and Doing Research in Applied Linguistics. He is also an editor of the journal, System. Before moving into academia, Jim taught in a range of diverse contexts including the US, Australia, Japan and Uganda.

### Advisory Board

Brian Paltridge, *University of Sydney*
Gary Barkhuizen, *University of Auckland*
Marta Gonzalez-Lloret, *University of Hawaii*
Li Wei, *UCL Institute of Education*
Victoria Murphy, *University of Oxford*
Diane Pecorari, *City University of Hong Kong*
Christa Van der Walt, *Stellenbosch University*

### About the Series

This Elements series aims to close the widening gap between researchers and practitioners by allying research with language teaching practices, in its exploration of research-informed teaching, and teaching-informed research. The series builds upon a rich history of pedagogical research in its exploration of new insights within the field of language teaching.

## Cambridge Elements ≡

# Elements in the Series

*Language Teacher Educator Identity*
Gary Barkhuizen

A full series listing is available at: www.cambridge.org/ELAT

Printed in the United States
by Baker & Taylor Publisher Services